PERFECT SERVICE:
CREATING THE BEST HOTEL IN NEW YORK

```
TX
911.3
.M27
B673
1994
```

A prereleased edition of this book was published
in 1993 by Victoria International Corporation.
It is here reprinted by arrangement with Victoria International Corporation.

English edition copyright © 1994 by Magna Publications, Inc.
All rights reserved. Printed in the United States of America.
No part of this book may be reproduced
(except in the case of brief quotations embodied in critical articles and reviews)
in any form by any means without written permission
from Magna Publications, Inc.

Magna Publications, Inc. books may be purchased
for educational, business or sales promotional use.
For information, please call or write:
Hospitality Information Publishers, Magna Publications, Inc
2718 Dryden Drive, Madison, WI 53704.
Telephone: 608/246-3591; Fax: 608/246-3597.

Design: Tamara L. Cook
Copy Editor: Jenny Hofmeister

ISBN: 0-912150-32-7

For Annie

CREDITS

Much of the inspiration for this book came from my family. Nancy, my wife and partner, has been an extraordinary help to me in clarifying concepts and ideas. As a professional educator and producer of slide shows and videotapes, she has both an inquiring mind and the ability to simplify complex concepts. My children, Victoria (a new PhD in education), Teresa (a dining room manager), Natalia, Andres (a hotel restaurant manager), Ana Gabriela (a server at Bertuccis), Annie (who has a promising career in health care), and Peter (a rower and investment advisor), have been wonderful and supportive friends throughout our lives together.

Inspiration for this book has also come from my partners in Victoria International Corporation and the Freeman Group. Joseph Dennis, David Archibald, Vera Mae Wills, Nicky Lee, Nan Rubin, William Meister, Allan Wee, Janice Casey, Marke Hammond, Linda Chin Lee, Kathi Ransom, Harriet Burgoon Miskell, Lawrence Chin, Evelyn Tan, our late beloved Richard Rochon, Aliya Tealdo, Gail Healey, Suzanne Devlin, Ed Pendergast, David Warburg, Rick Mott, Liu Bai Fang, Bill Freeman, K.T. and Susan Phua have each helped to formulate the process described in the book. I am equally grateful that they carried our firm through the months it has taken me to research and write it. They are a widely respected group of professionals who served as a model for the "trainers" in the book. Like Nancy, they have also contributed endless creativity and fun to my professional life. Three of our former partners should also be mentioned. They are Mary McGlinchey, Stephen Monk and Virginia Jacobs.

When I wrote about Mr. Steiner, I thought about my own mentors and I would like to acknowledge a few of them. Each was patient enough to teach me skills and knowledge of the "real world" variety. They include Georgia and Bill Delano, Gerry and Warren Ziegler, Luis Munoz Marin, Fred and Carmen Wale, Robert Kennedy, Dr. Efren Ramirez, Laurance Rockefeller, Richard Holtzman, Nik Klotz, Fred Eydt, Hans Keller, Joel Jennings, Richard Hartman, Walter Vickers, the late Peter Hollaus, Marshall Thurber, and Robert Reid. I would like to thank Dr. W.E. Deming, whose magnificent seminar I attended in 1988 and whose lectures, books, and tapes have helped so many of us begin to clarify an extremely complex and far-reaching concept of service management for the next century. He, along with Stephen Covey, Phillip Crosby and Joseph Juran, will have an enormous influence on quality in the service industries. A special tribute should be paid to O. Lee Duff and Measurement Systems International. There is no doubt that Lee and his able and fun-loving partners, Dr. Gary Kaurman and Dr. Robert Frost, will help us figure out the next steps.

Finally, it is important to mention a few of the pioneers who are helping to guide the Quality Movement in the hospitality and health care industries. I am proud that many are my colleagues. They include Emily Richardson, Eric Nussbaum, all my fellow members of the AH&MA Quality Assurance Committee, Len D'Costa, Rolf Hartmann, Brian Joiner, Yuji Tsutsumi, Phil Lee, Leon Lee, Katsunori Antoku, John Cameron, Dr. Judy Lim, Sim Kay Wee, Leong Siew Loong, Dorothy Riddle, Carl Kono, Dr. Wayne Weiner, Peter Thompson, David Boyd, Darryl Chai, Larry Nishikawa, Nan Palmer, Peter Sholtes, Ruth Counts, Teddy Aoki, Song Jia, Elmer Coppoolse, Charley Park, Joe Doll, Barbara Whelan, Eugenia Hamilton, Zhang Xin Shen, Michael Bice, Kate Lalk, Judy King, Mary Reedy, Steven J. Shriver, Bai Zucheng, Cindy Clark, Jim Varnum, Bruce Glass, Dr. Paul Batalden, Dick Wright and Larry Rockefeller among many many others. Each has an open, inquisitive mind and each is contributing to the future.

With special thanks to Jean Guo and her late husband Tao Yu Tong.

In your work and my work we can become agents of profound change.

But nobody can predict the dimensions or directions this change will take.

We have only each other, our spirit, and our collaborations to guide us through the trackless forest.

The Cast in Order of Appearance

Lorna Johnson
General manager

Wilhelm Steiner
Lorna's mentor, now retired to Marbella

Sarah McCredie
Sales and marketing director

Sam Thompson
Controller

Walter Steinhager
Food and beverage director

Fred Hamel
Personnel director

Bill Holtzman
Training manager

Ruth Schmidt
Executive housekeeper

Joan Dieterle
Rooms division manager

Brian Foley
The catalyst, a consultant

Johnny DelGado
Union representative

John Wolcott
Owner

Simon Elliott
John Wolcott's lawyer

Chet Bertram
Engineer

Andy French
Executive chef

Maria Luisa Wolcott
Owner's wife

Meredith and Francesca
The Wolcott's daughters

Table of Contents

    I. Prologue 1
   II. Odyssey 5
  III. Inkling 19
  IV. The Owners... 21
   V. Group Grope.. 27
  VI. Genesis 33
 VII. The Program 37
VIII. Annie's Story 43
  IX. Long Look.. 49
   X. Commitment 53
  XI. Long View.. 59
 XII. Brian's Lecture..................................... 61
XIII. The Chain of Service 73
XIV. Innovation.. 83
 XV. Who Are We and
       Where Are We We Going? 87
XVI. Driving Force 93
XVII. "Facilitator" 97
XVIII. Homecoming 111
XIX. Meetings... 115
 XX. Training... 117
XXI. Leadership 121
XXII. The Gathering................................... 123
XXIII. The Renovation................................ 131
XXIV. T.I.G.E.R. 135
XXV. Harmony... 139
XXVI. Graduation 141
XXVII. Sweet & Sour 147
XXVIII. Statistics, Beautiful Statistics............ 149
XXIX. The Mirror 155
XXX. Clean, Well-Maintained Rooms 159
XXXI. Coffee Shop.. 163
XXXII. Housekeeping's New Tricks............ 167
XXXIII. Triumph... 171
XXXIV. Author's Note.................................... 175
XXXV. Epilogue 177

vii

chapter I

Prologue

By 9 p.m., Lorna Johnson felt that she had been pushing pieces of paper from one side of her desk to the other for her entire career.

Her mentor, Wilhelm Steiner, had always told her to keep a neat desk so that any guest walking in would feel that he or she had Lorna's complete attention. She dutifully kept a neat desk with an enormous pile of paperwork hidden away in one of the drawers. Each time she pulled it out, she had to sort through the entire pile to find the report or letter she was looking for. She suspected that Mr. Steiner did the same thing.

Lorna was exhausted. She had been up at 5 a.m. to tour the hotel, had eaten a brief breakfast with some of the night cleaners in the employee cafeteria, met with the chief engineer at 7:30 and sat through a second "power breakfast" with the station manager for Lufthansa, whose business she had been after for months, at the insistence of the regional sales office.

She had met with her executive committee for three hours. The meeting had been interrupted by calls from the regional office and the home office. Normally, she tolerated no interruptions, not even from guests. But her bosses at Palmer Hotel Corporation had always been excepted.

The executive committee meeting had been frustrating and inconclusive. Sarah McCredie, the sales and marketing director, and Sam Thompson, the controller, had engaged in a pitched battle over some of the salespeople's expenses. Overtime continued to be a problem, for reasons no one seemed to be able to explain. Walter Steinhager, the food and beverage director, had complained bitterly about his budget, saying it had been prepared by a nincompoop who had no idea of how to run a first-class New York hotel. Fred Hamel, the personnel director, had been furious that the rooms division manager was letting Ruth Schmidt, the executive housekeeper, hire without following the format which all had agreed upon; that is, letting personnel prescreen applicants first. Fred was a little touchy anyway, as one of his latest hires had apparently walked out with a new laser printer. The training manager, Bill Holtzman, had been upset because only three people had shown up at the corporate-mandated "Guaranteed Happy Guest" course the previous day.

Joan Dieterle, the rooms division manager, had looked at Lorna toward the end of the meeting and said, "What do you want — guest satisfaction or no overtime? We hadn't budgeted for all the training 'Guaranteed Happy Guest' was going to require. I don't think anyone in the home office knew it was going to be so expensive. *You have to decide.*" (A phrase Lorna heard at least twenty times a day.)

Five guests managed to reach her with complaints about room charges or disappearing laundry. With some she was tough and with others gentle. She knew that if she gave too much away it would show up in the regional office annual audit. Each meeting was time consuming, but Lorna knew that she had a way with difficult customers that some of her managers lacked. They either became antagonistic or gave away the store. Subsequently, she insisted on dealing with difficult guests.

Lorna missed lunch because one of the smoke detectors went off on the tenth floor, and a guest called in to report that someone had stolen her two thousand dollar necklace. Palmer Hotel corporate policy stated that the senior manager-on-duty should investigate both.

She had also been informed by the regional office that they needed a report for the owners the following day. It seems the owners were concerned that plans for the renovation of the fifth floor were running way over budget and over a month late. "Only a month?" thought Lorna to herself.

At 7 p.m., after another brief meal in the employee cafeteria with Johnny DelGado, one of the union representatives, she had finally been able to get to the office to attack the report for regional.

Perfect Service

But first she had to wade through a pile of memos, mostly generated by her own staff, and complaining about actions taken by others, few of which had to do with guests. Steiner had been a master of memo writing but detested the process. "This is the American way to run hotels," he would say disdainfully.

Then she started writing her report on her secretary's computer. The regional office had been horrified that she had ordered her own computer.

Just as she finished the report, the door opened. A small gray-haired man in an expensive but rumpled suit stood staring at her. Lorna tried to conceal her surprise and irritation. "Yes?" she asked.

"I am giving a seminar in your hotel in the morning and I just wanted to find out which room we're meeting in," he said apologetically.

Lorna brusquely asked for the details, deftly pulled out the function sheet and from a pile of papers gave him the information.

"You've had a tough day, I'll bet," he said.

She really looked at him for the first time. He seemed to actually mean it. "If you had an hour and needed a good cry, I'd tell you about it," she said, not altogether pleasantly.

Much to her surprise he offered to buy her a cup of coffee. Lorna checked on the meeting room for him, put on her beeper, and walked with him over to the coffee shop.

chapter
II

Odyssey

His name was Brian Foley. He was a management consultant. He was sixty-four years old and a grandfather. He had been a quality control manager for twenty-four years before taking up consulting (when he and 6,000 other people had been laid off from his factory in the Midwest). "When you are fifty-four and jobless, you become a consultant."

This is all she found out about Brian directly because for the next two hours he asked questions and listened.

And for two hours Lorna talked. Steiner had taught her that loyalty was next to godliness in the hotel business, and she felt a twinge of disloyalty. Brian, however, was clearly discreet. He would not even tell her who his clients were or what he did for them.

In response to his questions, she began hesitantly. "I went to the University of New Hampshire Hotel School. I wanted to be near my mother in Boston and I thought I wanted to be in the hotel business. I went to work for Palmer Hotel Company right out of college as a management intern. My first boss, Wilhelm Steiner, was a general manager who genuinely wanted me to succeed. I later learned that many others are primarily concerned with saving their own skins."

In Lorna's eyes, Steiner had been a traditional hotelier who had taught her that "the devil is in the detail." Obsessive about details, he toured the hotel at least twice a day. He did not hesitate to gently remind each staff member of their duties when they seemed to be lagging. He kept endless notes to himself on his staff's commitments. He followed up on everything. He personally remembered what every VIP guest liked and sent them personal notes on birthdays or Christmas.

As a manager, his style was characterized by gentle ruthlessness. He demanded perfection from his staff and fired senior staff members when they failed to fit his mold. When they performed, however, they became part of his family. He protected them from outside intervention, particularly from corporate, which he viewed as an outside annoyance. "What do they know about hotel business?" he once said in a quiet moment of frustration. "Call them on Saturday morning some time. You don't even get a recording." He worked incredibly hard and he expected everyone else to do the same. He measured dedication in terms of hours worked. "The guests aren't here nine to five and neither are we," he once said.

Lorna adored working for Mr. Steiner. He took a grandfatherly interest in her and her internship. She decided early to ignore some of his somewhat outdated ideas about her gender, such as, "Women will never make good general managers — they are too emotional," or "Work hard and it will help you find a good husband, but don't marry a hotel man!"

Her first year with Steiner had been one of constant motion as she was shifted from one department to another. One week she would be washing dishes, the next she would be night auditor. "Don't trust the computer," said Steiner. "Check the figures yourself. Computers are the problem, not the solution."

Every week, no matter how full the house, or how big the crisis ("Hotels without crisis are about to go bankrupt," Steiner said), he met with Lorna and the other two interns and debriefed them.

By the end of that first grueling year she became aware of a depressing fact. One by one, her U.N.H. classmates were dropping out of the hotel business. One called it a torture chamber. "We're hired for mileage," he said, "and I'm out of gas." Another had added up the hours he'd worked and concluded that over his career, he would earn the equivalent of five dollars an hour. "More disturbing for some was the intangibility of the hotel business," she told Brian. "It got to them that the rules were constantly changing. There was no continuity. Everything appeared to depend on the whim of the manager in charge. The wheel got reinvented each morning."

Lorna, however, thrived. She had always enjoyed working hard and been proud of the hours she put in. No two days were alike and she enjoyed putting out fires.

Perfect Service

At the end of a year of internship, Steiner asked her to decide what area she would like to focus on. She chose food and beverage, feeling that she did not fully understand its complexities. She also noticed that most of the Palmer general managers came from food and beverage. At this point there was a slight disagreement with her mentor. He felt that although marriage was not imminent, at any moment it could strike like lightning and end her career. He felt that she should focus on sales, front office, or housekeeping, where women could fulfill their promise and move more rapidly. Steiner even drew her a chart that showed her that her lifetime earnings would be much higher as executive housekeeper — if she didn't get married. She looked at some data (collected quietly within Palmer by what was called the "feminist underground") that showed while ninety percent of executive housekeepers were women, only four percent of food and beverage directors were women.

She finally asked if he might have a food and beverage position available that would enable her to continue working under his tutelage. Flattered by this request, Steiner created a position of assistant restaurant manager in the coffee shop.

The restaurant manager, Jacques Sauvage, was a tyrant who distrusted everyone. He looked at the world in terms of good guys and bad guys. When push came to shove, there were only two good guys, Steiner and himself. Everyone else was suspect. This particularly included Lorna, whom Jacques considered a serious threat to his relationship with Steiner.

Together, Jacques and Steiner had been through two major Palmer Hotel openings, including one in the Middle East. "At least there the women don't try to take over," said Jacques. They had also been through three turnarounds where, at the request of the owners or lenders, Palmer had taken over a hotel in serious trouble. Palmer was known for its ruthless turnarounds, which included firing all "non-compliant" (a term Jacques applied very liberally) employees from all levels, if the union situation permitted.

Jacques judged the world at large by a hierarchy he had invented in his mind. While the European male ranked near the top, the American woman was near the bottom.

Jacques was a poor teacher, even by hotel standards. He taught by correcting mistakes in public. At times his obsequiousness toward guests and bosses was in direct conflict with his disdain toward the employees. He would snarl quietly at a staff member while apologizing to a guest in the same breath. When Lorna suggested a training program, his reaction was entirely negative. "They should know," he would say. "It's just common sense," or "You have to be flexible, use your head."

7

Perfect Service

It took a little while for Lorna to get accustomed to Jacques. He reduced her to tears several times and embarrassed her (several times in front of Mr. Steiner). She never let her tears nor her embarrassment show in public, but, nonetheless, she was deeply hurt by Jacques' behavior. The coffee shop had a very high turnover of staff, even for Boston, which was suffering from about seventy percent turnover of staff for the hotel industry overall.

His toughness, loyalty and obsequiousness to his superiors stood him in good stead in the regional office. He was praised for his efforts, particularly for keeping his costs way down. Although the restaurant was not very profitable, Lorna noticed early that Palmer did not seem to expect to make a profit in its restaurants. "How could so many non-hotel restaurants in Boston do so well?" she asked herself.

Only Lorna's New England grit and ability to work long hours got her through those first few months in the coffee shop. She had little responsibility. She tried to write down the procedures for the three meals served in the restaurant so that she could train the new staff. But she found that Jacques would change the way things were done from one day to the next. He always hired experienced wait staff from other hotels. He would eat at the restaurants around town and leave his business card and a large tip with a "good" waiter.

Jacques controlled everything in the restaurant at all times, so that Lorna often was running errands instead of managing the staff. This did not stop him from blaming her when things went wrong.

Even Steiner was unsympathetic. "Trial by fire," he said. "You can't fight success and Jacques is very successful." He also did not want to undermine Jacques' authority. Thus, Lorna felt rejected by her boss and her mentor at the same time.

Her classmates were sympathetic to what she was going through. Many were going through the same grist mill. By the end of the second year, nearly half had quit the hotel industry.

Lorna was working incredible hours. The restaurant was open from 6 a.m. to 10 p.m. and there were times when she felt that she was covering all hours for all days. "I had to work hard to learn from Jacques," she told Brian. "I realize now that he was very threatened by me, but the idea that a twenty-five-year-old person still green around the gills could be a threat to a forty-five-year-old professional with a proven track record would have been completely strange to me at the time. I guess because I was a threat, he was very reluctant to teach me anything.

"My mother was wonderful to me during this time. My father had been killed early in the Vietnam War and my mother had supported my sister and me ever since. She is a manager herself at Prudential and she understands a great deal about people. 'Flatter him,' she said, 'but be honest. Don't praise him for qualities he doesn't have.' And flatter him, I did. This allowed him to be more patient with me for the moment, but he needed constant reassurance. It was very tiresome to have a forty-five-year-old child.

"At the end of my second year with Steiner, he felt that I was ready to move on as a dining room manager in a smaller hotel. He had established an incredible network with other Palmer managers. They all spent a great deal of time on the phone with each other and knew what was happening at corporate headquarters and in the regional office. I realized later that Steiner's placement of me was a carefully thought out strategic move on his part. He placed me with a manager named Kevin McCarthy in New Orleans. The hotel had three hundred rooms and a relatively sleepy coffee shop. The hotel was doing modest business in a poor market. Because it was exceeding its owners' expectations, they were not second-guessing Palmer every moment.

"Kevin was young and tough," Lorna said. "He was able to chart his own course while appearing to be within the strictly defined limits given him by the regional office.

"When I took over the coffee shop, although it appeared to be well-run, it was actually in a shambles. Food costs were high. Beverage sales were low. Wine sales were nonexistent because the wait staff were intimidated by wine. The staff had set up their own system, which meant that there was a great deal of specialization. 'That's not my table, dear,' or 'You'll have to give your order to Josey, I'm only the busboy.' Customers had to wait in line to get in the restaurant in the morning, when there were a dozen empty tables in plain sight. For all his foibles, Jacques would never have tolerated these problems. Certainly he would have never let the staff set up the schedule, steal each others' orders, ignore guests, and fail to ring up an occasional cash sale.

"There was virtually no turnover of staff in this coffee shop. To me, the constant turmoil of the Palmer Boston Hotel was preferable to the lethargy and deviousness that existed in the Palmer New Orleans Hotel."

Kevin was aware of the problems. "This is a real challenge for you. The whole place is out of control," he said. "The first thing is to show them who's boss."

"It's not what you expect, it's what you inspect," said Kevin. Lorna took this very much to heart, asking questions, observing and correcting. It was the first time in her career that she had been in charge, and she took everything very personally. If Lorna gave an order and it wasn't obeyed, she became hurt and angry. For six months she was angry all the time. She found herself subconsciously emulating Jacques, thinking somehow that his style was going to bring the same control she had seen in his restaurant.

"The union filed continuous grievances against me," Lorna told Brian. "I lost a few because I blew my cool a couple of times and said or did things which I regretted."

"Kevin said, 'Don't get angry, get even. Don't let them upset you.'

"As if I could control my emotions," added Lorna. "At this point, I felt that I was ready to get out of the business. My classmates were right. Only masochists and incompetents could survive in the hotel industry! If anyone had offered me a job, I would have taken it, except for one factor. I was failing. My stubborn streak would not let me quit while I was failing. So I hung on."

Lorna continued, "The New Orleans food and beverage director was aloof and unapproachable. He was a complete snob. He had no use for the coffee shop and focused his entire effort on the gourmet restaurant Maison LaFitte. He also personally catered gourmet functions for the elite business and social crowd of New Orleans. The coffee shop, its customers, its staff and its managers troubled him not.

"Once, in an executive committee meeting, Kevin had asked how the coffee shop was coming along. 'The coffee shop is the coffee shop,' sighed the food and beverage director. 'What more can I say?'

"I began burning up the long distance lines to Boston, talking to my mother. The hotel business was very strange to her but she was a good listener. I suppose that's what I needed."

Lorna continued, "My goal in life at that time was to break the back of 'the mafia,' a group of coffee shop employees who, in my opinion, led all the others. They were tough middle-aged women who were syrupy sweet to the customers and uncompromising to management. If you tried to change their schedule, they would all call in sick and those who were to replace them on their shifts would call in sick. They stretched the limits of the union contract as far as they could. They knew that managers came and went. The average coffee shop manager in Palmer stays in one place twenty-six months before moving on."

Lorna was surprised that Brian seemed to be astonished at this. "That's no exaggeration," she said. "Some other hotel companies are proud that the average managers move so fast that they never stay in one place more than eight months. Hotel school graduates are trained to think that moss is growing under their feet if they don't move on every few months. The mafia knew this, of course, and ran their own shop. Life to them is an intern program, a work study assignment."

At Kevin's suggestions, she finally called a meeting with all the coffee shop staff and invited the hotel union shop steward. Her intention was to lay down the law with everyone at the same time, rather than get nibbled to death by the individual employees. The issue she chose was a change in schedule, an issue within management's rights. The schedule had been worked out years before by a particularly compassionate coffee shop manager to ensure that the mothers among the wait staff could get home in time to meet their children in the afternoon. Those same mothers never worked weekends. Lorna, in consultation with the hotel's labor lawyer, determined that the schedule could be changed regardless of seniority.

Lorna presented a schedule under which each mother was to work every third weekend. One of the mothers exploded, accusing Lorna of being a "complete fool." "You have no idea what the guests want, all you care about is brown-nosing Kevin." (They never dared call the general manager by his first name to his face.)

Lorna finally blew up. "Since the moment I walked in here, you've been giving me nothing but grief," she shouted. "I don't want this job. You're making me miserable...." Now everyone was shouting. For Lorna, all the anger and frustration and fear of failure that had been nagging her came out.

The meeting went on for an hour and a half. Maria, the leader of the mafia, finally agreed to a new schedule, but wanted to discuss the schedule with Lorna in advance each time it was posted. Lorna remembered one snippet of conversation when she had exclaimed, "Who runs the coffee shop, me or you?" "You do, but you can't do it without us," stormed Maria. "Sometimes I'd like to try," Lorna said.

For some reason the union shop steward held back. He did not add to the shouting and confusion. In fact, he began to serve as mediator, clarifying the points of view of each side. He intervened quietly, helping them reach a compromise whereby Lorna would review hardship cases.

When the meeting was over, Lorna felt elated, even though she had not bent them to her will, and for some reason the staff seemed to feel equally triumphant. They had somehow come to understand each other better. Against her better judgment, she even accepted an invitation to a barbecue. The food and beverage director accused her of "going native."

Lorna felt, however, that she had never gotten the coffee shop under control. "It was one of my greatest failures. There were some improvements, but as soon as I left, they reverted back to their old ways."

Another formative incident was the opening of the Palmer Dallas Hotel. She mentioned it in passing, but Brian asked her to elaborate. Lorna asked him why.

"In an opening of a new facility the corporate culture is on display," Brian responded. She asked what corporate culture is, but Brian did not

11

answer.

Palmer Hotels had developed a system of opening hotels, which was to bring in a task force from other Palmer hotels to supplement the permanent management staff to supervise and to train. New employees, most of whom were stolen from other hotels, were trained for a period of three to ten days.

Lorna was responsible for training at the hotel's gourmet restaurant. She found out about the assignment a week in advance, which gave her a little time to study the operations of the Maison LaFitte restaurant in her own hotel. There were no written standards and procedures to study, so she observed the service in the dining room and talked with the staff. She felt totally unprepared to train people in such a complex process.

The opening was exciting and chaotic. One day there were contractors everywhere, a week later there were guests everywhere. She found that she enjoyed training enormously. The staff was highly motivated. Not only was it a new building, but a new opportunity.

The work was hard. Lorna had to make many decisions fast. The restaurant manager was not particularly strong and he let her decide service procedures (usually on the spot). The general manager and food and beverage director ignored the restaurant until two nights before the opening, when there was a "trial feeding" (a full dress rehearsal). Both planned to dine in the restaurant and had asked Lorna and the restaurant manager to join them. She drilled her two most experienced wait staff all afternoon and felt prepared.

The general manager was a nitpicker and found fault with everything. The food and beverage director joined in, not to be outshone by his boss. The wait staff, sensing things were going poorly, became flustered and made a number of foolish mistakes. The general manager's meal was sent back with a cynical comment.

Lorna felt completely deflated. She was confused because while they had talked about things they didn't like, such as the method of table side service and the presentation of some of the food items, they gave her very little guidance as to what they *did* want.

She spent a sleepless night and toward morning decided to confront the food and beverage director to find out exactly what he did want. She made a long list of questions, and sought him out in the coffee shop early the next morning.

"I was fascinated by your ideas last night," she lied, "and I wanted to hear more about them. Could we talk now for a couple of minutes?" They talked for over an hour and she was able to go through the entire checklist.

"How do we make sure that the general manager and the regional food and beverage director also agree to this?" she asked, feigning innocence.

"In this particular barnyard, I am the rooster. Trust me." said the food and beverage director.

She met with her weary and depressed trainees and dining room manager at noon, and they went through the list. The afternoon was spent rehearsing the changes in service and Lorna invited the food and beverage director in for a second meal.

He made several more changes, but this time he focused mainly on the presentation, calling the chef to his table three times during the course of the meal. The service staff was relieved to have the heat put on someone else.

The final night before the opening of the hotel, the general manager and regional vice president of operations ate in the restaurant with one of the owners and the mayor of Dallas. Lorna was nauseous from anxiety before the meal. The dining room manager had somehow pulled a disappearing act all afternoon, leaving her to prepare the staff. Some of the changes had forced them to borrow some equipment from one of the other hotels in town.

When the party arrived, Lorna personally greeted them, seated them, and stayed within twenty feet of the table the entire evening, while the dining room manager covered the other tables.

The meal was a triumph and one of the owners praised Lorna for her training job, offering her a toast.

Brian interrupted Lorna's tale, "Does everyone agree that this is the best system for opening a hotel?"

"No," she laughed. "Some managers call it the 'pigeon system' — the task force flies in, leaves droppings all over the place and flies away. But it works, and corporate says, 'If it ain't broke, don't fix it.'"

"I'll bet there is high turnover of staff with that system," Brian said, "and I'll bet the dining room manager didn't make it."

Lorna looked at him quizzically. "I won't take that bet." she said. "He was a loser. But, the important thing was to get the property open."

"Property?" Brian looked confused.

"Our owners are primarily in the real estate business," Lorna said. "Palmer Hotel Corporation is a caretaker, hired by those owners to maintain and enhance the real estate value. Palmer only owns a few hotels." Brian seemed to be turning this over in his mind, so Lorna returned to her story.

From coffee shop manager in New Orleans, Lorna was promoted to assistant food and beverage director in Anaheim. She was beginning to develop a reputation within the North America Division as a go-getter. The regional food and beverage director felt that she had all the essential qualities for success; loyalty, a hard worker, a quick learner, and a good company person. The turnover of food and beverage management staff was horrendous in the region, and within six months Lorna was promoted to food and beverage director in a medium-sized, high-volume airport hotel in Denver.

She had a tremendous opportunity to star at the Palmer Denver Hotel. The general manager was interested primarily in the rooms division. Like many hotel general managers, he viewed food and beverage as an amenity, not as a profit center. The only direction was up.

Lorna was beginning to realize that her weakness as a manager was accounting. Budgets were developed by the controller in most Palmer hotels, and managers were often stuck with rigid and unrealistic budgets. The controller in Denver was young, open-minded and extremely ambitious. So, she paired with him to master accounting, and soon the two began generating numbers that would make the regional office take notice.

First, they made the restaurants exceed budget by cutting staff and food costs, and by building revenue through some advertising and promotions whose costs did not come from the food and beverage budgets. Unused capital and creative bookkeeping added more money. They created instant success.

"The experience taught me how to generate great numbers," she told Brian. "I was amazed at what happened once I understood a little bit about the accounting process. I also realized that the general manager himself hardly grasped the meaning of the numbers and viewed accounting as some mysterious and evil force."

Next, Lorna and the controller analyzed every possible source of potential revenue. They found that there was tremendous potential for banquet and catering business in the airport community. On her own, Lorna developed gourmet box lunches that were sent out to an executive jet service. These became very popular and highly profitable.

Now the regional office really took notice because they always liked to be able to pass on success stories to the corporate office and good numbers were the sweetest news of all.

"Palmer is owned by CTX Corporation, is it not?" asked Brian.

"It sure is," Lorna said. "And the board members are either Palmer people or CTX people, no outsiders.

"The board meets once a month," she continued. "Some corporate people spend two weeks a month recovering from the last board meeting and the other two weeks getting ready for the next. Unfortunately, lots of people in CTX have a very strong interest in Palmer and the company is overrun with MBA's with sharp pencils.

"Palmer, particularly now, has a real bug in its ear about quality. CTX is only very slowly beginning to think about quality, but believe me, when a headquarter's financial person calls up and complains about overtime, the guest had better be ready for slow service or a long wait to get into his room, because that call is being generated right out of CTX."

"It sounds like you were beginning to understand your own company quite well," Brian said.

"I sure was," she agreed. "John Eydt, the controller at Denver, used to talk about the 'three of great facts' of life. The first great fact was that financial numbers are *the* critical measurement of a hotel's success; absolute numbers, comparative numbers, percentages, year-to-date, numbers against budgets, cost of sales, inventory numbers. That was the way CTX could understand the business.

"John's second great fact was that few people in a hotel have any mastery of numbers. Executive committee members are constantly being ambushed by their controller, the regional office, or the general manager for numbers they do not understand, create or feel in control of. The customer is always right, but the P&L is 'righter.'

"His third great fact was that you could generate wonderful numbers in a short time and *for* a short time. You could defer projects, cut services, drop rates, slash costs. All of these could have a dramatic impact during the length of time one seemed to be in one place and would leave an incredible mess for the next person to clean up."

These three facts, she had realized, could do wonders for her future.

The Denver numbers pushed Lorna's career into high gear. Within ten months she was offered the job of resident manager in Houston. She visited the property and realized that anything she could have done had already been done, and the market was terrible. The Denver formula would simply not work. She turned down the job in Houston, claiming that she had not completed her objectives in Denver. This was a risky strategy, but it had a positive impact and even further enhanced her reputation. "This woman is generating great numbers, and she really sticks to her program. She even turned down a promotion."

"Did you feel that you were becoming a little cynical?" inquired Brian.

15

Lorna paused. There was an embarrassed silence. "I guess I feel that I have a role in the industry," she said. "You have to pay your dues and learn the rules. Here I was being handed the rules. I wasn't going to fight them, no matter how silly they sometimes seemed to me. I also wanted to be known as a team player, not a maverick."

Four months after she turned down the Houston job, she accepted the resident manager position in Atlanta.

Atlanta was a dream job. She had a brilliant, but frustrated controller, and a classic European-trained general manager who was intimidated by the entire financial process. His department heads were young and aggressive but felt stifled. The general manager, at the end of his career, was content to let Lorna run the day-to-day operations of the hotel, which she did carefully but with great enthusiasm. She quietly unloaded deadwood from the middle management structure and put two department heads on notice, watching their departments like a hawk for some misstep on their part. She earned a reputation with the union as a tough negotiator who did her homework. She generated a number of grievances but managed to win most of them. And she took care of the details, the V.I.P.'s, and the regional office.

But above all, she watched the numbers. She was probably the first resident manager in the region to put a computer in her office. It was tied directly into the mainframe in the controller's office.

She took several courses and even learned how to set up her own financial programs. She and the controller personally developed the budgets for the hotel, and it was no coincidence that they brought their numbers in ahead of target.

Despite guest complaints and sagging employee morale, the general manager was pleased to bask in the corporate limelight. And the regional office took an unprecedented step. When the general manager retired a year later, they asked Lorna to take over the property as acting general manager.

Lorna was now putting in sixty-hour weeks but enjoying it enormously. She began to push her occupancy numbers ever higher by promoting the hotel to the group market. She made several very successful deals with airlines, undercutting her rivals.

"Were all your numbers showing an improvement?" asked Brian.

"No. Two numbers troubled me. One was repeat business and the other was the average room rate. Both were showing a gradual decline. I simply could not keep the rates as high as they had been. The hotel was badly in need of renovations and two new all-suite hotels opened up nearby. I think this had more to do with the problem than anything else. The other numbers were so good that both the owner and the corporate office agreed with my conjecture."

She had soon been promoted to general manager in Atlanta, the first woman general manager, and at thirty-two, the youngest in the region. The property was billed as a major example of a turnaround.

Two years after her arrival in Atlanta, Lorna was promoted to take over the Palmer Madison Avenue Hotel in New York. The hotel was in the upper middle range in terms of facilities and rates. It was not a group hotel, but appealed to individual business and tourist travelers. The rooms were nice and the restaurants had a fairly good reputation, although they were not particularly popular with the local crowd.

Lorna felt very ambivalent about New York. The regional office was right down the block. The New York guest was tough and insatiable, and the employees seemed to be cut from the same cloth.

On the other hand she knew that there was great truth in Frank Sinatra's song about making it in New York. And the numbers looked great. The hotel was consistently running 85 percent occupancy, with a high average room rate. Upon reviewing the hotel's numbers, she found a great deal of fat in the payroll and other cost areas. "Walk softly and carry a big set of scissors," advised the regional controller.

During the six months she had been in the hotel, she had hardly walked softly. She had managed to get rid of four department heads who were not carrying their weight. She had even gotten rid of one of the replacements. She had put a very tight control on the overtime and food costs, and she had tried to duplicate the Atlanta plan for the rooms and the Denver plan for the food and beverage department.

"It sounds like a success story," Brian said.

Lorna sighed. "Some days, I feel like I'm back in New Orleans," she concluded. "I feel like I am wading in molasses and that it's me against them. I can see now how Jacques Sauvage got the way he did."

"You feel you don't know who to trust," ventured Brian.

"Understatement of the year."

Lorna was beginning to feel true exhaustion, but prompted by Brian's intense interest, she talked a few minutes about the general state of the hotel.

"You're a wonderful listener," Lorna said, "and I probably said a lot of things I shouldn't have. Now, I'd like to get *your* opinion of all this. As a consultant, do you find this situation here normal?"

"I don't know anything about the hotel business, so what I say would have no base of experience. But I would like to suggest that none of these conditions need to exist. Things do not need to be the way you describe them. I suspect that you have learned to accept premises in your work that are basically false," Brian said gently.

Lorna was aghast. She felt hurt by the comment. "All the best managers in my region would agree with me and so would the best managers of other hotel corporations," she protested.

"A friend of mine once had a brilliant idea," Brian continued. "He went to four different patent attorneys in Boston and each one told him that the idea was unworkable and unprotectable. Finally, he believed that they were right and pushed his career in a different direction.

"Someone else made the same discovery and got rich. Lorna, lots of people can share the conventional wisdom and be wrong. I have no doubt that you play the game brilliantly, but are you playing the *right* game?"

chapter
III

Inkling

The conversation was deeply troubling to Lorna. Her career in the hotel industry seemed to be composed of a series of unpredictable peaks and valleys. She pushed just as hard when things were going well as she did when they were going poorly. Yet the same strategy that worked brilliantly in one time and place would backfire in another. There were rules, but then there were no rules. Her mother was not even much help anymore because the hotel industry seemed so strange to her. She described it, to Lorna's dismay, as "a land without justice."

Brian was working with a group of senior executives in an aerospace company for three days in the hotel. Lorna watched the group from a discrete distance and noticed that their obvious tension and discomfort was diminishing during their stay. On the third day, she dreamed up an excuse to talk with the company's chief executive officer, Mr. Pitkin, regarding the facilities.

"I am the hotel's general manager, Mr. Pitkin, and I just wanted to make sure your stay is going well."

"It is going very well," he said, "and your staff has been very helpful."

"How are your meetings going?"

"We've been working with this guy, Brian Foley, for over three years now. It's been very satisfactory," Mr. Pitkin volunteered.

"Three years! He must be doing good work for you," Lorna remarked. And slowly, she thought to herself.

"Changing your market position takes time, but we've become the best in the industry," he said.

"May I ask why you needed an external consultant?"

"It's a very good question and I don't mind answering it. People within the company are carrying around too much emotional baggage. An outsider can see through all that. And besides, Foley has a lot of specific experience in improving quality."

"There must be pressure on you as a CEO to solve the problem yourself," remarked Lorna.

"Change is survival in our industry," he smiled. "It's like nature. When the ice age comes, you have to move south. I have two problems. First, I am convinced that I must change my role from manager to leader. Foley's helping me personally figure out how to do that. Secondly, he's helping us, as an organization, confront very complicated changes in our industry. I would be dumb not to seek outside help. My own parent company recommended it."

"What about the cost?"

"We allocate ten percent of our budget on training for ourselves, our staff and on outside consultants. This is one part of our budget that stays the same, no matter how tough times are. This meeting is costing me seventeen thousand dollars. I can assure you it will add fifty thousand dollars in value to our operations. But that's not the point. If you don't stop and bite into the future, it's going to bite into you."

"You must be in a very supportive corporate environment."

"Hardly, but they accept the facts."

Upon concluding this conversation, Lorna hurried back to her office, dreading her next meeting.

chapter
IV

Owners
the

The Wolcotts were a wealthy New York family. John Wolcott represented the third generation, which sometimes had strained relations with their parents. The older generation was usually represented by trust lawyers from an old New York firm. The lawyers didn't do much to create peaceful relations.

The primary goal of these lawyers was stability. They did not enjoy presenting bad news to the rebellious members of the family's third generation. They also tried to keep the family separated from day-to-day involvement in its own investments. Most of the lawyers were contemporaries of the older generation, a generation no longer active in the business affairs of the family but who were distrustful and indeed threatened by John Wolcott's generation. Ironically, the members of the third generation were now approaching middle-age themselves. The older family members looked at the lawyers as a way of protecting their money from the impulses and capricious ways of the "hippies," as some of the third generation were referred to privately.

Lorna disliked the family's lawyers, who were incredibly stuffy and patronizing and constantly inferred that Palmer Hotel Company was not giving the family, and their retainers, a fair share.

All in all, there were three members of the second generation still alive and seventeen members of the third generation. The twenty-eight members of the fourth generation were all under twenty, and Lorna hoped that she would be long gone by the time they became actively interested in the hotel.

John Wolcott was a forty-year-old Harvard MBA who was sharp and totally distrustful of the lawyers. His wife, Maria Luisa, was also an MBA and equally astute. John and Maria Luisa had always taken an interest in the hotel, and, on John's insistence, had established a first-name relationship with Lorna.

Lorna treated the family and the lawyers with respect and reserve and said as little as possible in the meetings. She knew that owners could mousetrap an unsuspecting manager and torpedo a management contract. She envied one of the other Palmer general managers who had an agreement with his owners that they would not even come in the hotel without his permission.

John Wolcott and one of his father's lawyers, Simon Elliott, were waiting for Lorna in her office. After pleasantries were exchanged, Mr. Elliott said somewhat patronizingly, "Mr. and Mrs. Wolcott would like to play a more active role in the family's New York real estate holdings. They would like to institute a monthly review of this hotel's operations. This review would constitute a meeting with you and other staff as needed, as well as a thorough study of all financial data. We have studied our contract with Palmer and there is no language that prevents our doing this."

John made a few conciliatory remarks and added, "We would also like to meet occasionally with a group of the employees selected randomly from various departments. They would be selected by us from the staffing list."

Good God! thought Lorna, they don't trust Palmer and they don't trust me. The staff is going to figure this out and hamstring us.

"This seems like a very good idea," she remarked with feigned enthusiasm. Thinking quickly she added, "I will, of course, need to review the idea with the regional office. If they agree, I'd like to suggest that the invitation to line staff to attend a meeting come from me rather than directly from the owners."

"Of course," said John, before Mr. Elliott could speak.

They proceeded to review the renovation project and last month's P&L. Mr. Elliott pointed out that there had been no financial improvement since Lorna had taken over. "I can not say we are not a little disappointed," he concluded.

What a royal mess, Lorna said to herself after they had left. By mid-afternoon she realized she was deeply troubled by the Wolcotts' apparent lack of confidence in her capabilities.

With her heart pounding and a severe headache, she picked up the phone and called John Wolcott. She had been discouraged from doing this by regional, but he seemed the sort who would never let them know. After some small talk, she said hesitantly, "John, I was a little disturbed by our meeting. It sounds as though you're worried about the hotel. What seems to be the problem?"

"Well, Lorna, I'm glad you brought it up. Maria Luisa and I have been a little unhappy about the direction the hotel's taking." Alarmed, Lorna asked, "Well, where would you like to see the hotel go?" After a pause, John spoke, "I probably speak only for Maria Luisa and myself, but we would like to have the Palmer Madison Avenue Hotel be known as the best hotel in New York. We really don't know why it can't be. The location is good, the rooms can be very nice. Yet some people don't rate it even in the top tier."

Lorna let this sink in. "Off the record, are those my marching orders?" she asked. "Off the record, yes," he said firmly.

At 8 p.m. that same evening, Lorna was again staring with unfocused eyes at a pile of paper when Brian walked cheerfully into her office.

"We've had a good experience here, but I was wondering if I could offer you a couple of suggestions for handling other groups like ours?" he asked.

From force of habit, Lorna stood up and offered Brian a chair. Hiding her weariness, she grabbed a pen and piece of paper. Brian talked very specifically about several aspects of the hotel's service that had not worked well.

Lorna tried to find out who the people were who provided the service, but Brian ducked specific reference to individuals. "Don't try to nail individuals, Lorna, think about the system," he said. "The system drives the individuals." Lorna paused, "I thought it was the other way around," she said slowly.

Brian leaned back in his chair, "Well, for example, there are no wall outlets outside of our meeting room so you have to use sterno heaters instead of electric for the coffee and hot water. The staff cannot be reasonably expected to run back to check the heat of the coffee urn every twenty minutes. If the coffee is not hot, you could blame a waiter, I suppose, but the system is working against the waiter.

"Another example is the linen. The laundry is not in operation on

Sunday, I'm told. If there are lots of banquets and meetings over the weekend, you must often run out of linen for the tables on Monday. Whose fault is that?"

As he was leaving, she asked him how he would approach work at a hotel as an outside consultant.

"Very carefully," he replied, smiling.

"Seriously," she insisted. "I'm beginning to think we could use a little help. You really shook me up the other night and I think there may be some truth to what you said. And God knows we do have some difficulties."

He paused for a long moment.

"Possibly, but there are a couple of things I should clarify," he said.

"First, I would need to know the company and the industry a great deal better than I do now. I could not ethically charge you for my whole education. Secondly, I would want to have a contract for at least three years. I do not believe in instant change. Change is usually painful, expensive and time-consuming. Most important, it begins with a change in mindset and that is a slow process in itself."

"Three years is longer than I have ever stayed in one job," Lorna said.

"Maybe it's time you changed that habit. But even if you leave, my contract is with the organization, not the individual. I would keep working."

"What do you charge?" asked Lorna.

"Fifteen hundred dollars a day," Brian said, "and I normally work a minimum of thirty days a year for one client."

The cost seemed astronomically high to Lorna. For only a few days a year of Brian's time, she could pay the price of a well-trained, full-time operations analyst.

She had enough presence of mind to trade business cards with Brian, and Brian agreed to send her a proposal.

"When I take on a new client, I ask ten questions during the course of the first few months. Whether you work with me or not, you might think about them." He wrote the ten questions in a neat longhand on a scrap of paper.

Perfect Service

BRIAN'S TEN QUESTIONS

1. What do you do? What is the mission of your organization? What business are you in?

2. Who are your customers?

3. How would you like the organization to be described in ten years?

4. What are rules that guide the organization's behavior?

5. What are the organization's key factors for success?

6. What are the attributes that your customers consider most important in your business?

7. How do your customers rank these attributes?

8. What barriers prevent you from meeting these attributes?

9. What can you do to overcome these barriers?

10. What are the focal points?

chapter

V

Group Grope

Brian's proposal came in the form of a two-page letter of agreement two days later. Lorna agonized for a few days. Finally, feeling she was going to need a lot of help, she signed it and sent it back with an initial retainer check, cut by a mystified controller. Brian would begin work a month later.

Lorna had once seen a movie on how to run a meeting. The movie had nothing to do with how she had seen meetings run in hotels. In fact, she and the other managers who had seen the movie thought it was a joke. The executive committee meetings which she ran were modeled after the meetings that she had seen Steiner run. Fast and to the point, Steiner encouraged little participation.

Lorna had a pile of papers and went through them, handing them to the individual who had responsibility for solving the problem represented. She read a few negative guest letters and found out what happened from the people in charge of the areas in question.

She then asked Sam Thompson, the controller, for a report, which led to some mild bloodshed about who was overspending and why. Joan Dieterle, rooms division manager, summarized the forecast. The engineer summarized safety activities. (This was mandated by corporate decree and usually took less than a minute with no discussion.) The personnel director, Fred Hamel, listed the job vacancies and then Lorna asked each person if they had any announcements. Lorna carefully wrote down who said they were going to do what, to remind them of their commitment at their next meeting. The meeting usually took less than an hour and there was very little participation. When there was discussion, it was generally an open battle, which she usually ended with a decision.

Lorna was absolutely certain that raising any philosophical questions such as the ones posed by Brian would lead to a lessening of her authority. Each manager felt he or she was being paid to make decisions on his or her own operations and Lorna was being paid to make decisions on the overall well-being of the hotel. Accountability meant decision-making. If you were accountable for an operation you were responsible for deciding how services in that area were rendered.

A question such as, "What is our mission?" seemed nebulous and unimportant, as well as dangerous. If it were important she would be expected to go to the mountain and look under a burning bush for the answer. The regional office was nearer than the mountain.

"Oh, by the way," she finally said near the end of the executive meeting, "Ford Motor company has a mission statement. If a newspaper reporter asked us what our mission statement was, what would you tell them?"

At first the group stared at her, faces blank. Then they began to warm to the question with facetious answers. Cynicism is a safe place to hide when in an uncharted territory.

"Never to have overtime," said Sarah.

"Assets always equal liabilities plus owner's equity," said another.

"Cover your tail," said Joan.

"Thirty-five percent gross operating profit," said Sam.

"Spoken like a true controller," said Walter, "but you're wrong; it's twenty-six percent food costs."

"Please the owner's wife," said Chet Bertram, the engineer.

They gradually realized that Lorna was asking a serious question. She read them the Ford Motor Company mission statement.

Perfect Service

FORD MOTOR COMPANY

STATEMENT OF MISSION

Ford Motor Company is a worldwide leader in automotive-related products and services as well as in newer industries such as aerospace, communications, and financial services. Our mission is to improve continually our products and services to meet our customers' needs, allowing us to provide a reasonable return for our stockholders, the owners of our business.

There was complete silence. Lorna was not sure how to interpret it.

"Why did Ford write a mission statement?" asked Fred.

Lorna herself was not sure. "They needed direction," she suggested. There was some perfunctory discussion.

She felt the meeting was not getting anywhere. She was uncomfortable herself with the subject, and it was clear that the group shared her discomfort. Steiner had told her never ask a question unless you already have the answer. The problem was that they were problem-solvers, and a mission statement was not a solution to a problem, at least the kind of problem they could sink their teeth into.

However, Sarah McCredie, the director of sales, somehow missed the overall cynicism of the group and began to become excited about the idea. "Our mission," she said, "is to be the best damned hotel in New York."

Lorna breathed a sigh of relief, but almost immediately, the group turned on Sarah.

"When our owners won't spend twenty thousand dollars for new bathroom fixtures?" Chet asked.

"When our ballroom is the size of the maid's closet at the Marriott?" Bill questioned.

"And every time we book part of a city-wide convention, the hotel looks like hurricane Edna had passed through."

Sarah looked at her watch.

Lorna saw that she was quickly losing ground and did not know how to regain it. However, the thought of facing Brian empty-handed appealed to her even less than continuing the meeting.

"Let me ask you another question," she said. "What do you see as the key factors for success as a business?"

"Meaning what?" asked Joan.

"What advantages do we have over our competition?"

"Who is our competition?" queried Sam.

"Other hotels in our price range, I suppose." Ouch, she thought. I should have been more positive and had an answer ready for that one, and I should have asked the questions in order.

"Location, I suppose, although it is not as good as some of the others," mused Joan.

Sarah was coming back to life. "Location for whom? We're in a great location for the theatergoer."

"And the X-rated moviegoer," said another to nervous laughter.

"So, is location an advantage or not?" asked Lorna.

"What do you think, Lorna?"

"I guess it is, as Joan said, particularly for some of our guests."

She looked at her bewildered executive secretary, Martha, who was not sure what to put down.

"Put down location."

"Under what, the payroll report?" asked Martha.

"Just put it down, I'll explain after the meeting."

Martha dutifully wrote the word on a clean sheet of paper.

"What else?" demanded Lorna. She was going to persist even if the process was more trouble than it was worth. In the movie there were lots of ideas from around the table. In her meetings there was never any discussion. When there was any interchange, it was usually in the form of a put-down.

"Room size," said Fred.

"Maybe, but the Marriott has much bigger rooms."

"So does the Hilton."

"Size."

"Size? We're the smallest hotel in our category."

"That's what I mean. I think that gives us an advantage. The Marriott, the Hilton, the Grand Hyatt and the Sheraton are huge."

For the first time there was a real discussion. In fact, there was a free-for-all. Everyone talked, no one listened. Once a member of the group decided on a position, she or he dug themself in. There was no way of getting them off their position.

While the debate raged, Lorna daydreamed. The idea of a small hotel intrigued her. She herself preferred the smallest size hotel possible. A Vermont country inn was just fine for her. The same person that checked you in served you dinner.

She was annoyed by people who rated your success in the business by the number of rooms you managed. She often found herself getting defensive, insisting that although she had two hundred and thirty rooms, she ran ninety percent occupancy.

What about creating a little inn out of her hotel, an inn that would appeal to rich Japanese and European guests? Forget it, corporate and the owners would never permit it. And there was too much competition, too many other people trying to do the same thing.

She noticed abruptly that people were looking at her out of the corners of their eyes, expecting her to come up with the answer.

"Put down small size," she said, ending the meeting, and the group filed out of the room. She singled out Sarah and asked her to stay.

"I'm sorry you got jumped on for sticking your neck out."

"Don't worry, I learned my lesson," said Sarah. "I also learned not to count on you to stick up for me."

Lorna was taken aback. She felt that Sarah was being totally unfair to her. In a way, she had stuck up for her.

"Listen, we are both under time pressure," she said, "Let's get together for a drink late this afternoon, around seven. Is that OK?"

"If you say so," said Sarah.

Lorna walked back to her office simmering with anger; anger at her staff who seemed petty and childish in a serious discussion, anger at Brian who had asked her to bring these irrelevant subjects into a business meeting, and angry at herself.

Our focus is only on each other, she thought. We spend an enormous amount of time meeting with each other, writing memos to each other, and thinking about each other. What about the rest of the staff, the regional office, the corporation, the owners? What about the guests?

chapter
VI

Genesis

Brian called a few times during the month to give Lorna words of encouragement, which she sorely needed. She did not bring up his ten questions with the executive committee again. And she sometimes felt she had made a mistake in hiring him.

His first full day working for the hotel was the twelfth of July. Unfortunately, there was a large check-in for an incentive group that day, accompanied by a heavy epidemic of no-show/no-call employees. The plan was for Lorna to spend an hour with Brian and then have him meet with each member of the executive committee. She was only able to give him fifteen minutes. The other meetings were constantly juggled during the day, and Brian had to cool his heels for at least two hours. Despite the pressures, most of the executives seemed to enjoy talking with Brian. Lorna had told them that he was discreet, that he would not reveal what they said individually, and that they could feel free to talk with him.

None of them believed a word of this, but Brian had a way of instilling confidence. During the next four days, Brian conducted meetings with nearly seventy of the employees in small groups and spent a great deal of time reviewing personnel data with Fred Hamel.

Lorna was half an hour late for a wrap-up meeting with Brian at the end of the week. She apologized.

"Remember," he said smiling, "you're paying one hundred eighty-five dollars an hour for my services, whether you're late or not. I would recommend that we quickly get to the point where the meetings begin on time. I'll always end them on time." He said this in a friendly way, but she knew he meant business.

"The problem is, we can't control the guests," she said lamely.

"Nor should you. But you are managers as well as hoteliers. There seems to be a difference. Managers have some control over their time because they have staff dealing with their customers. If managers don't trust the staff or the customers don't trust the staff, that's a problem for management to work out. Otherwise, managers end up doing staff work."

"Point made," she said. "At least in theory. Well, what did you learn?"

Brian looked down at his notes. "Before I got here, I spent some time trying to understand your industry and your company in particular," he paused. "You are in a difficult situation if you seriously want to improve the quality of your product.

"First, let's talk about Palmer Hotel Corporation. Your chairman is apparently a pure hotelier. He is very concerned about quality and feels that quality will sell rooms. He is surrounded by people who have been raised in an adversarial and insecure environment. The politics of survival seems to be an important motivator in your company. Some of the very people in the corporation who could help produce the quality the chairman wants are finding themselves constantly distracted by power politics. Apparently, most hotel companies have the same conflict between short- and long-term needs.

"Another problem is that your parent company, CTX, has established a monthly financial review process that puts tremendous pressure on Palmer to produce a monthly quick fix for any problems that come up. This is natural; they are not hoteliers. They have to produce good news for stockholders who also are not hoteliers. The result is unfortunate. It means that long-range, slow-moving projects are going to play second fiddle to short-term band-aid solutions. Your region is headed by people who must spend a great deal of their time feeding this animal.

"I say all this because you seem to want to 'stabilize the process,' as we say in manufacturing. You must, however, be aware that the environment you work in does not support your goals.

"Now, let's talk about the hotel. Normally, the kind of change process I work with has the blessing of the senior people in the organization. This hotel is a twenty-eight million dollar business, owned by an individual but managed by the subsidiary of a manufacturing company. CTX is only going to support change that doesn't cost anything.

"Several members of the executive committee told me of your mission discussion. The idea of being the best hotel in New York appeals to only two of them and even they are intimidated by the idea. How do you feel about the idea yourself, Lorna?"

"I'm for it," Lorna said, looking him straight in the eye.

"Is it possible?" he asked.

"I hope it's possible! I'm under unofficial orders from John Wolcott to do exactly that — create the best hotel in New York. It's a mandate that seems a little overwhelming," she admitted.

"Do you feel you have the physical plant?" he inquired.

"Yes, but it needs a lot of attention. That's why the owners are considering a renovation," Lorna said. "The way I see it, the whole process depends on John Wolcott."

"What about your staff?" asked Brian.

Lorna thought for a moment. "They are cynical and worn out. Some of them have worked here forever. They're crusty with the guests. We have a new guest relations program that made a small dent in their attitudes, but not much. Ideally, we would close down, get rid of the whole lot and start over."

"They're all bad?"

"Obviously not," she said a little testily. "Some are quite good and most of them show up to work in the morning."

"Where you want to go is the most important decision you can make," Brian said slowly. "You can only achieve this mission by aligning your manager, staff and owners on a plan to get there."

Brian reviewed more of his observations with Lorna. Some of what he said stung her. They agreed that his next step would be to return in two weeks and conduct a questionnaire survey of the entire staff. He would present his findings to the executive committee two weeks after that.

Lorna realized Brian was taking her mandate seriously, and she found that each time she talked about it, she began to take it more and more seriously herself. She was also experiencing an almost mystical feeling of clarity.

chapter
VII

*P*the *rogram*

During the last week in July, Brian surveyed the entire staff of the hotel, interviewing other managers individually and most employees in small groups. He also administered a written questionnaire to all employees. The questionnaire was carefully designed to determine the needs of the employees and to determine whether management was meeting those needs. After reviewing the results, Brian created charts that showed the particular gaps between needs and expectations.

On a whim, Brian interviewed one summer intern on videotape. The interview gave the viewer a candid picture of how an entry-level employee viewed the hotel.

In mid-August, Brian met with the executive committee for the entire day. He spoke quietly and evenly. "I know the kind of pressures you are under, but once in a while it pays to take a long view. Sometimes it is not irresponsible to let your subordinates worry about the hotel for a few hours. You have responsibility for the day-to-day operations of the hotel, to be sure, but you have also been vested with a more important task and that is to safeguard the future of the hotel. Conditions change rapidly in our world and today's success story can be tomorrow's disaster."

He gave them several familiar examples of companies that had been high flyers one year and bankrupt the next. "These organizations simply did not think about the future. They received all the signals and chose to ignore them. None of them should have been surprised by what happened.

"Lorna hired me to help you focus on the future and prepare for it. We have a simple task. We must look at our present condition and compare it with where we would like to go. The gap between them is where we are going to focus.

"You have a vision: This is to be the best hotel in New York." Sarah's jaw literally dropped. Brian wrote "The best hotel in New York" on a flipchart. He repeated the concept several times.

"The best hotel in New York. It has a nice ring to it. Lorna, please come up here and ask the group what constitutes the best hotel in New York."

Lorna stood reluctantly and walked slowly to the flipchart. "It means repeat business." she said. "Great," encouraged Brian, "write it down on the flipchart. Now, ask the group what being the best hotel in New York means to them and write down the answers."

There was a long awkward silence. Sarah mumbled something.

"Speak up," Brian said to relieved laughter from the group.

"Sorbet."

"Great. Write it down, Lorna," Brian said.

"I don't even know how to spell it."

The list grew and the group, initially cynical about the exercise, slowly dropped their reserve and stopped looking to Lorna for approval for each item.

"Overnight shoe shine."

"Outrageous room rates."

"The Ritz Bar in Boston."

"European customers."

"Longer average stay."

"Nice customers."

"Immaculate rooms."

"Business center."

The list grew to several pages on the flip chart.

Brian stood and wrote "Barriers" at the top of a clean page. "What are the barriers that prevent you from attaining this goal?" he asked. The group proceeded to list some of the barriers. The list was extensive and a little depressing to the group.

"Money."

"Interference from corporate."

"The owners."

"The staff."

"Do you feel you can overcome these barriers without the assistance of the staff?" asked Brian.

"Obviously not," said Walter Steinhager, the director of food and beverage. "They are our greatest asset," he added piously.

The group continued listing barriers. Finally, Brian, who had been taking notes, stood up. "We have a simple job," he said. "Overcome the barriers."

"Simply impossible," murmured Walter.

Choosing his words carefully, Brian began talking to them. "I would like to share with you some observations and some recommendations for a program to help you effectively attain your goal and eliminate some of these barriers."

"First, some of the results of the surveys. As you know, the purpose of the questionnaire was to find out what the staff needs from management and then determine if you are meeting these needs. Please interrupt me if you have a question."

He proceeded to list the results of the survey.

Brian walked over to the flipchart and turned a few pages. "It is fundamental that an organization's effectiveness is based on how well it meets its beneficiaries' needs. Who are your beneficiaries? Your guests? Palmer Hotels? Your owners? Your employees?

"When the hotel can meet the needs of all its beneficiaries, the organization is aligned. Creating a quality workplace means creating a quality workplace in the eyes of the people who live in it. Quality is really the perception of quality provided in relation to perceptions of needs.

"This chart shows your staff's perception of their needs and it shows their perception of whether those needs are being met. These seven needs were determined by your staff to be most important." He turned to the chart.

INDEX OF SATISFACTION

NEEDS BY PRIORITY   (100 PERCENT = PERFECT)

1. Recognition for work well done 65%

2. Compensation and benefits (including duty meals) 54%

3. Knowing what is going on 46%

4. Having someone listen to me 50%

5. Knowing what is expected of me 72%

6. Knowing how to perform my job successfully 65%

7. My supervisor understands me and is concerned for my future 42%

"You can see that some of these needs are not perceived as being met," he said. "Some specific comments — first, more than half of the staff feel they don't have enough information to do their jobs effectively. They rank this as one of their highest frustrations.

"For example, several employees say they don't know about group business early enough to be able to plan. Others said they are unaware of financial performance. They are told that they should control costs but they don't know what those costs are, and they have no idea how well the hotel is doing in its revenues. Fifty percent felt that they don't know their schedule early enough to be able to plan their personal time.

"A high percentage felt that job assignments are unfair and that managers play favorites. This may also be a function of poor communication. By the way, only three out of the eighteen departments have meetings on a regular basis with their employees."

At this point Chet Bertram, the chief engineer, interjected, "How the hell can we meet regularly when we have a hotel to run? You can't predict when a toilet is going to clog up. You tell the guests they can't use the john because the engineers are in a meeting."

There was general assent.

Brian let the storm rage for a few minutes. "It sounds like a tough problem," he said finally.

"More like impossible," replied Chet.

"It's not a problem, it's an opportunity," said one of the group to general laughter.

"I've heard that concept before," Brian said, "and I always wonder what happens when you have an insurmountable opportunity. Among ourselves we are going to call problems problems and hope they are opportunities as well.

"Two questions," he continued. "One: Is part of your job to keep people informed and to find out what they are thinking about? And two: Can't you do this more efficiently in a meeting?

"If the answer to these questions is yes, then you and your employees are in agreement. You simply have a problem of logistics."

There was a glum silence. Two people nodded.

Brian continued, "A second major problem area is that employees don't feel their jobs are well-defined. For example, a dining room manager arbitrarily changes a procedure during meal service and embarrasses an employee in front of her guests and peers. A new manager arbitrarily changes a billing procedure without explaining why to his staff, except through a terse memo that I myself found hard to understand."

"Wait a minute," said Fred. "We have job descriptions for everyone."

"I know you do because I've read them," Brian said. "Remember, perceptions are reality.

"Furthermore," he continued, "there is virtually no training taking place at any level, except a little training for new employees and training that is mandated by Palmer Hotels Corporation. During the past year, employees attended, on the average, only four hours of formal training and most of them saw no value to that training.

"Many people feel that supervisory roles are not clear and that they are not well-prepared for promotions. Over half of your supervisors were promoted from within. None attended a course before they were promoted, and only a few have been given training on the basics of supervision since promotion."

Brian looked around the silent room and back down at his notes. "The third major finding is that employees need, and don't feel they are getting enough, recognition in their work. About half felt that they would like to know more about how they are doing from their immediate boss."

"Nobody in this business gets a lot of that," said Ruth Schmidt, the executive housekeeper. "They should know that."

"How many of you would like to know exactly how you stand with your boss?" asked Brian.

Lorna's hand shot up, followed by everyone else's hand.

Brian concluded, "You will have to ask a great deal from your employees in order to become the 'Best Hotel in New York.' A basic rule I follow is if you want to motivate people to meet your needs, you have to first meet their needs.

"Now, I would like to show you a short videotape of Annie Baldwin, who was a summer intern and who was kind enough to let me interview her about her experiences. Joan," he asked, "she worked in your department. How did she do?"

"She was excellent," said Joan, "always cheerful and very good with the guests."

"Would you hire her again?"

"Yes, definitely," Joan answered.

chapter
VIII

Annie's Story

Brian turned on a tape deck and Annie appeared on the TV screen.

ANNIE: I was hired for a summer job.
I guess they take on several kids every summer.
I'm going into my second year of college at U. Mass and was thinking of going to the hotel school. This was a great chance for me to see how I felt about the hotel business.

BRIAN: Do you think you would like to have a career in the hotel business?

ANNIE: No way!

BRIAN: Why don't you describe your experiences and how you felt about them.

ANNIE: I was hired as a reservations clerk, but I was told that I might rotate to the front desk and the PBX if I did well in reservations.

The first morning I met with the front office manager for about three minutes. He was under a lot of pressure and he had interviewed me, so I guess it didn't make sense to him to spend a lot of time with me. He did ask me if I had any questions.

How the heck would I know if I had any questions? My mind was one big question. The biggest question was, "Will I survive?" and I didn't want to ask that. I was introduced to one of the reservationists and she gave me a beat-up, old three-ring binder full of memos. I read through them all morning but really didn't understand what they said for the most part. There were a lot of abbreviations and terms I had never heard before. I had a pad of paper and I wrote them all down and asked her for clarification between calls. She was helpful, but kept saying it was simple after a while. I still don't agree with that. In the afternoon, she let me take a reservation, but after a few seconds she jumped on the line and took over. By the end of the day, I had only taken one complete reservation and felt more confused than ever. If I didn't have to face my dad, I would have quit.

I gradually learned how to take reservations. Dorothy would listen in and point out what I did wrong. She's a real nerd, you know what I mean. She's nice and all but not very expressive. She never told me I was doing a good job.

Another way I learned how to do the job was to look on the bulletin board. The board had the famous Palmer service standards and some other stuff. One thing on there is a big crayon sign that tells what to say when you answer the phone. It says: ALWAYS SAY GOOD MORNING (AFTERNOON, EVENING), THE PALMER MADISON AVENUE HOTEL, RESERVATIONS OFFICE, (NAME) SPEAKING, AT YOUR SERVICE!

Another one says: THE PHONE MUST ALWAYS BE ANSWERED WITHIN THREE RINGS.

You know, they never bring people on before they need them, never. This is a real pain, because you need the new person the moment they arrive, and you don't have time to train them because you are trying to cover for their dumb mistakes. Right now they're short on the front desk and could use me, but they're also short on the switchboard. It's all because they are trying to cut down on payroll. But who wants to work in that kind of place? So people leave and you perpetuate the problem.

Sometimes the person doing the training is new and doesn't know much. I got a real airhead training me on the front desk one day. He never let me do anything. When the guest had a question, he would interrupt and answer. He would contradict me in front of the guest.

Another thing — They never let you know if you are doing well. As far as I know right now, I didn't do a very good job.

You would get little reminders, though. Once in a while, the front office manager would be listening in and he would tap his fingers on the sign on the bulletin board if you did not follow the routine exactly as written. Of course, then you'd get rattled and do all kinds of crazy things. It was really insulting.

When I trained for PBX later on, I got very good training from Alicia. She was patient and wanted me to be successful. She was good with the guests and the other workers but she was very rough with some of the supervisors and managers. She got fired halfway through the summer for her attitude. She said they were keeping a file on her and she didn't give a damn anyway. I liked her a lot. She was a real leader among us.

Another person who started when I did was fired before the probationary period was up because her grammar was not very good.

BRIAN: How often did you meet with your boss?

ANNIE: The reservations manager used to come by about once a week and sit down with me and say, "Talk to me." But I wasn't sure what she wanted me to say. I wanted to tell her about a lot of things, but once, when I made a suggestion, she got defensive and after that I shut up. We never met with the whole front office staff or with just the reservationists.

BRIAN: Would that have been useful?

ANNIE: I think so. Definitely, because then we could have all voiced our likes and dislikes. The front office manager could have taken notes and taken our problems to his boss. I heard though that they didn't listen to him anyway. They just said that's your problem, you deal with it.

I can tell you the atmosphere was really poor sometimes. You didn't feel that management really cared about you. Management reminds me of people at parties who ask you questions only so you can give them a chance to talk.

BRIAN: Can you give me an example?

ANNIE: Sure. Last Saturday morning, the front office manager was somewhere in the hotel. He was on duty. I was working at the front desk where I had been training all week. A guest came to check out and complained to me about the rate. The guest was supposed to pay one rate, according to the computer. But she had an ad that showed that she was supposed to pay a different rate. She was furious with her bill and told me I had to change it.

I had never seen the ad, but she had it right there. I tried to reach the manager and he didn't answer his page. The guest just stood there and glared at me. Finally, she went out to lunch and told me she would be back later.

The manager showed up two hours later. I was really upset and asked him where he had been and then he got upset and snapped back at me. He asked me why I didn't call him on his beeper. I didn't know he had a beeper. No one had ever told me how to reach him. "Anyway," he said, "give the guest the lower rate."

BRIAN: Should you have had the authorization to set the rate?

ANNIE: No, I would never want that.

BRIAN: Why?

ANNIE: What would happen if I made a mistake? Management would be all over me.

BRIAN: Have you been a member of other teams beside this one?

ANNIE: Yes, we had an intramural volleyball tournament in our dorm during orientation week. Everyone was required to play and everyone helped each other out and encouraged each other.

BRIAN: What happened if you made a mistake?

ANNIE: The coaches applauded and encouraged you so you would try harder. You have to take chances in volleyball, like serving overhand, or you'll never get to be any good.

BRIAN: Couldn't a hotel be run like this?

ANNIE: It's too serious in a hotel. It would never happen. The managers can't allow mistakes. Anyway, after he snapped at me, I had a fit and a half. I started crying and ran into the bathroom. I came back out in a really bad mood. He went up to Diane, one of the other workers, explained to her why he snapped at me and then didn't say a single word to me. Diane doesn't care why he got mad at me.

BRIAN: Did he ever apologize for the situation?

ANNIE: No. Everyone there is such a baby. No one can be wrong. And then Sunday he said, "Hi, how are you doing?" and then tried to complain to me about the other managers. I don't care about that. I just want to do a good job. I mean, that's the point, isn't it?

Another problem is that the supervisors don't always set a good example. One of them, Carol, forgets how to run the computer. A couple came in to register last week and she said, "Oh, you're not in the computer!" We knew they were, but she had forgotten how to pull out that kind of reservation. A couple of times we have seen her chew gum in the front when she's checking in guests. I mean, you wonder how she ever got to be a supervisor.

Sometimes I think the whole hotel is set up to be selfish. The union is greedy and selfish, management is greedy and selfish, and the employees are greedy and selfish. And the employees, who could be the real leaders, who love working with the guests, who have lots of ideas, leave after a while or put their energy in other things. It's really sad. Nobody really feels successful in their work.

chapter
IX

Long Look

There was silence in the room as the tape ended. Finally, Lorna asked, "Is that what you mean by the system, Brian?" "Exactly," he said.

"Maybe the system needs a new front office manager," said Joan.

"It would be easy to blame the front office manager," Brian said. "However, he is a product of the system himself."

"I would like to share with you some observations and recommendations," he continued. "Overall, there seems to be a diversity of purpose between you and the line staff. They seem to be overly concerned about their own creature comforts and the quality of work life and you seem overly concerned about controlling them.

"You are spending an inordinate amount of time trying to impose your will on your staff and they are spending a great deal of time resisting you. This is expensive.

"The result is polarization between the 'good guys' — management, and the 'bad guys' — the staff, and the bad guys outnumber the good guys by a six-to-one ratio. Thus, your position in a test of wills is hopeless.

"Secondly, the systems you do have do not seem to serve your guests. It takes the average guest eight minutes to check out even though the actual check-out process on the computer takes less than a minute. The reason for this is that the guests are standing in line for at least seven minutes.

"In accounting, to give an example, you have a policy of an automatic thirty-day delay for a rebate to a guest. This helps you guard your cash and means greater accuracy in the process. How does it help a guest, however, to have to wait a month to get their own money back?

"If a guest claims that a shirt is ruined by the laundry," he continued, "you make them fill out a form and insist on keeping the old shirt. In a hotel I stayed at in London, the laundry lost my shirt. They asked me the color and size and a bellman delivered a new shirt to my door an hour later."

"We'd be buying shirts for every guest," muttered Sam.

"With the kind of guests you want to attract, you need to trust them," continued Brian. "Trust could give you a strategic advantage over your competition."

"Speaking of trust," he said, "you are spending a great deal of time and effort inspecting the work of others. There are four people in housekeeping who do nothing but inspect rooms. You have an expeditor in the kitchen who inspects every plate that comes out of the gourmet restaurant.

"This is expensive. It means that one out of six people in the hotel are spending their time checking on the work of others. If the others did their job right to begin with, you would eliminate the need for all of these people.

"Thus, the whole reporting structure may have evolved from a set of assumptions that are outdated and archaic. If, for example, you feel that the workers are not to be trusted, then you need people to check them. But how do you know the checkers are trustworthy? So, you have an executive white glove inspection to check the checkers. And Lorna ends up checking a few rooms herself."

"I'm damn glad I do," Lorna said, "because I always find a problem."

"But whose job are you doing?" asked Brian.

"The executive housekeeper's and the rooms division manager's."

"And whose job are they doing in the white glove inspection?"

"The floor supervisors'," Lorna said, "and the floor supervisors are doing the room attendants' jobs when they inspect rooms."

Brian nodded. "Finally, your focus seems to be short-term. To become the 'Best Hotel in New York' is going to take more than a month or a quarter or even a year. Yet your focus is getting from one relatively short period of time to another, as if one period did not build toward the next."

"What do you mean?" asked Joan.

"What are some of the most important numbers to the rooms division?"

"Occupancy."

Brian looked around the room. "Are you willing to sacrifice occupancy figures this quarter for higher room rates next year? Could you go for two years with a lower occupancy while your room rates gradually inched up? If I were your owner and understood the logic of how a sacrifice over the short-run would give me a much more solid market share, over the long-run I might be willing to go along for the ride."

"But you're not our owner," said Sam.

"If you all are willing to put your efforts into changes, I'm going to wish I were.

"Your measurement systems," Brian said, "and your system of rewards and punishments are not related to your customers. When I sat in on your executive committee meeting, the only discussion about customer needs and preferences were two: a reading of an unfriendly letter from one guest and the discussion of a group that was coming in.

"Much more of your time is spent on trying to control costs than on improving revenues and therefore, the quality of the services provided. You treat these services as a given. If they fall down, it's a matter of getting a new manager in or more motivation for your staff.

"If a manager is rewarded for cutting costs or controlling his or her inventory, that has obviously got to take priority over trying to figure out how to better serve his or her customers. In fact, the customers may well take second position."

At this moment someone brought a message into the room with a question from the regional office about a budget item. Lorna picked up the phone with a mild apology and spoke with the regional controller. The group waited patiently while Lorna defended a five thousand dollar item in the budget. It was a purchase of new vacuum cleaners for the housekeeping department. It seems that the union had brought the issue to her attention as had the room attendants with whom she met informally. The old vacuum cleaners had been inexpensive, but had limited power and broke down constantly. At the moment, only half were actually working, so that the room attendants had to share machines. She did not quite dare also mention to the regional office that she had rented some vacuum cleaners that morning and was burying the costs in another budget item. She ended up compromising and agreeing to reduce the item to twenty-five hundred dollars per year over a two-year period of time.

When the conversation was over, she looked at the group. There was a long moment of silence.

Sarah looked at Brian. "Is that what you mean?"

"It's part of it," he said.

chapter
X

Commitment

As the day wore on, Lorna could see that Brian had begun to have a major impact on the group. They were much more outgoing, even feisty, than she had ever seen them. She also knew that much of the group's argumentativeness was what happens just before people become convinced of a new point of view.

"I would like to conclude this session," Brian said, "by outlining my recommendations. I see us working as a partnership, combining our expertise and experience for the purpose of achieving your vision of the 'Best Hotel in New York.' This effort will take place over three years. The effort will be lead by Lorna...."

"If I'm here," Lorna said.

The group laughed. "If any of us are here," said Walter.

"Seriously," Lorna said, looking around the group, "would you rather stay put for three years and focus on one process, one incredible achievement, one that Brian calls 'transformation,' or move progressively into larger and larger hotels without ever knowing what you are capable of doing?"

"I would, but there is no guarantee that the regional office will buy it. Even if they do, they may not be here that long. We've had three regional vice-presidents in four years, each trying to make a splash in his own fashion," said Fred in a quiet voice.

"But you would prefer it," persisted Lorna. "What about the rest of you, would you like to focus your career on one process in one hotel for the next three years?"

"I would," said Sarah.

"So would I," said Walter.

"I would if you can stand me," said Joan.

"It sounds like Brian won't need me anyway," said the controller.

"You're avoiding the question. Are you in or out?" asked Lorna.

"I'm in. A little of what Brian says has a ring of truth to it," said Sam.

Brian smiled.

"What about you, Chet?" Lorna asked the chief engineer.

"Where else would I go? Seriously, I'm in if we can get some more renovation money out of the owners. Or, politely said, convince the regional office to get the courage to go to the owners to fix up the place."

"That's settled," Brian said. "Now, these are my rules: First, we adopt the view that people are basically good, that they are capable of greatness, and that the environment we create for them — the systems, knowledge, and skills — can bring out this greatness." He paused awkwardly. "I always feel funny when I say this because there is so much evidence to the contrary. But I have seen in Japan, and more recently in China, that focusing on people's innate goodness is an incredibly powerful management tool."

His audience shifted uncomfortably in their seats while Brian continued.

"Second, let us look at this so called 'transformation' as a process rather than a program. In other words, it's long-term. It's not a quick fix that will pump up the numbers or create a little instant notoriety for yourselves or the owners. Your staff will instantly sense a program, what they call 'the flavor of the month.'

"Third, we will need to be able to take risks and thus make major mistakes, which will be learning experiences. One company fires a cannon every time a major mistake is made. The more we try, the more often the cannon will go off.

"Fourth, we must be totally honest with each other, disagreeing and critiquing each other candidly. At the same time, we should support the process enthusiastically to our constituents, our guests, owners, bosses, and staff.

"Our open-mindedness must also extend to getting suggestions from our constituents," he continued. "So, my fifth point is that we must actively enroll, rather than exclude, our beneficiaries from the process. This includes members of the Wolcott family. In fact, rather than exclude them, I recommend that we actively include their involvement and educate them in the hotel business."

"Hold on," Lorna said. "I like the other points, but in a way you are asking the Palmer Hotel Company to work its way out of a management contract, which, by the way, is up for renewal in three years."

"That's a risk, yes," agreed Brian, "but I suspect, however, that it will go the other way. The more they know you, the more they are going to admire your talents and feel a need to continue the partnership."

Brian concluded, "If you accept these principles, we will need to live by them in our daily work lives and remind each other when they are not being followed."

He looked around the group. Bill Holtzman, the training director who had been silent up to now, said, "I feel comfortable with these, Brian. But they're going to be very hard to follow."

There were murmurs of assent.

Brian turned a page on the flip chart.

"I recommend," he said, "that we follow a four-step process."

1. Establish a new operational philosophy and strategy.

"Lorna has agreed that we will take the entire Board of Operations away for a weekend in October to develop a strategy."

He pointed to the next item.

2. Define standards and procedures from a customer/service standpoint.

Brian said, "By this, I mean to analyze all jobs from the standpoint of how they can most effectively serve the customer. Remember Karl Albrecht's key concept. If the employee is not serving a customer, he or she is usually serving someone who is."

"It also means looking at every step in the flow of service procedure and determining if it adds value to the customer.

"We will then establish a thorough training system for all staff in setting up standards and procedures. Depending on your personality," he continued, "this step could be the most enjoyable or the most boring because it will mean a lot of analysis and writing."

3. Measure the entire flow of services in the hotel.

"I know 'statistical process control' is a new concept for you," Brian said. "The purpose is to ensure that you constantly measure how you are doing in the eyes of your beneficiaries."

Sarah said, "But we have guest comment cards, and corporate has a system of sampling two hundred customers a quarter and giving us an index to show how we compare with the other hotels like us."

"I have looked at the system and it's a good start," Brian said, "but the sample is too small. You might have as many as twelve thousand different guests during three months and two hundred is less than two percent. Secondly, it's slow. You have to wait too long to get the feedback from the process. Third, the important comparison is not with the other hotels, but with yourself. From what I understand, Palmer's strategic advantage lies in being able to respond to local market conditions. Fourth, it does not discriminate between various market segments. I would suggest a faster and much more comprehensive system of measuring customer satisfaction.

"The advantage is that you and your constituents will know exactly how you are doing at all times and you will be able to anticipate the Palmer Happy Guest Index."

Brian pointed to the flip chart.

4. Continually improve quality.

"Once you have the processes under control," he said, "you and your staff should focus your efforts on constantly improving services to meet, anticipate and even exceed the needs of the customers. The most valuable input will come from the staff."

"That I doubt," said Fred. "I am sure they have some good ideas but they'll be discouraged from participating by the union."

"Let's see what happens," Brian said. "We'll talk a good deal about motivation. One of my theories is that participation itself is motivation. The unions in Japan in the early fifties were much stronger and more anti-management than your union and yet they ended up supporting total participation."

Brian pointed to the last line.

5. Create a quality work environment.

"In order to bring about the kind of transformation you want, it will be important to develop stability and consistency in the labor force. It will also be necessary to develop a reputation as the best place to work in the New York labor market.

"Although your turnover is not too high, it's costing you at least four thousand dollars every time a person leaves, particularly if you count lost revenue created by new employee mistakes. This turnover of staff is directly related to whether you are meeting people's needs."

Brian paused and asked for questions. There was a lively discussion in which Brian served as moderator, drawing everyone in. He remained calm and in good humor. Instead of defending himself, he would restate points made by others and ask for other opinions.

Finally, Lorna stood up and thanked the group for their comments. She summarized the next steps.

"Our weekend with the Board of Operations will be on October seventeenth. John Wolcott, you will be surprised to know, will be joining us. Please don't mention that to anyone."

Chet protested loudly, "Bringing him is a terrible idea. Nobody will say anything, Lorna. And the regional office is going to think you're playing politics."

"Why does the regional office even need to be involved?" asked Sarah. The group members looked at each other.

"They don't," Lorna said.

She continued, "In December, we have scheduled a trainer training session for the entire Board of Operations and the supervisors. Bill will brief you on this beforehand."

"Finally, in February, Brian will present a course called 'Service Innovation,' which will help us better understand statistics and the problem-solving process."

chapter XI
Long View

Lorna awoke early. The brilliant October sun slanted in through the window. The sounds of early morning crept through the old Vermont inn they had chosen for their two-day retreat. The building itself seemed to be alive. Here, legend held, Ethan Allen caroused with the Green Mountain Boys after planning their battles of succession from New York. Here, years later, Lafayette had stopped on his triumphant tour through the newly created United States.

A rooster crowed far-off. A woman sang somewhere in the labyrinth of rooms two floors below. A tailgate slammed on a pickup truck. A muted radio gave the weather and corn prices. Lorna dressed quickly and went down the narrow staircase. The ancient front door creaked slightly as she opened it. For a moment, she stood on the worn granite steps and then set off walking toward a nearby hill on a gravel road.

The air was cold. The leaves glowed red and golden against the bright blue sky. The hayfields, still green, were speckled with diamonds of moisture.

She drank in the beauty and solitude of the early fall morning. To think, to be on her own, to feel clearheaded seemed a luxury. The anxieties and uncertainties that pressed in on her daily working life had disappeared.

As she walked above the town, Lorna felt a sense of confidence in herself and excitement in her new task. This was a task of her own choosing, dictated neither by those above nor below her in the hierarchy. She remembered a conversation with Brian.

"If you are going to be an agent of change," Brian had said, "you have to take the long view; get away from the detail. Turn your back on the present and focus on the future."

"How do you do that?" she had asked him. Everything she had been taught about the job of the hotelier was to sweat the details. She quoted the chairman of Palmer Hotel Corporation, who said, "the devil is in the detail." Brian had judiciously remained silent, knowing she would discover the answer herself.

Until this moment, Lorna had felt that improving the hotel was just going to add to her daily chores. As she walked, she realized that in order to really help the hotel, she would have to depend on the team to take over many of its daily operations. There was no way that she could do justice to the program ahead of her and still spend as many hours as she formerly had on the day-to-day operations.

chapter
XII

Brian's Lecture

Brian began in a quiet, measured voice. The group quickly realized, however, that he had more than a passing interest in his subject. And his concern was broader than the hotel.

"My purpose this morning," he began, "is to expose you to both facts and ideas which may help change the way you look at your work, just as it has changed mine.

"When you undertake the task of transforming an organization, you are change agents.

"It is interesting to me," Brian commented, "how many similarities there are between organizations and individuals in their ability to adjust to change. Organizations, like individuals, can think strategically, capture the opportunities presented and attack the problem with confidence and excitement."

"On the other hand, both can retreat, lay blame, take a defensive posture, and squabble over details."

He paused, looking around the room. "The price of admission to the change agents' club is to be open to change yourself.

"For you personally, this is going to be tough. You are not at a point of desperation. You have been moderately successful, you are not yet in the crisis. You are getting very little external or internal pressure for change, except from Lorna. Your work habits, your skills have been useful to you and have helped you get as far as you have. Even though I sense each of you want to change, you will find it very hard to replace old thoughts and old ways of working with new, untested concepts.

"Today, I am going to talk about the following: the change process, motivation, the nature of organizations, and quality.

"Change in organizations is inevitable. External conditions are changing and internal conditions are changing. Give me an example of an external condition affecting the hotel."

"Pressures by corporate to improve guest satisfaction," said Bill.

"New hotels in New York," said Sarah, "and changes in tastes."

"Change in tax laws," Lorna said.

"Recession and fear of recession," said Andy French, the executive chef.

"What about examples of internal changes?" asked Brian.

"Building getting older," said Chet.

"Staff getting older," said Joan.

"Expectations of staff changing," said Ruth Schmidt, the executive housekeeper.

"The ability of organizations to respond to external and internal conditions determines their ability to compete," Brian continued.

"What are some examples of companies or organizations which have not been able to absorb change?"

"General Motors."

"The British Empire."

"Continental Bank."

"Eastern Airlines."

"The government of North Korea."

"IBM."

"Good examples," Brian said. "The great problem is that change is happening faster and faster.

"Eastern Airlines never made a profit after the airlines were deregulated. It was incapable of adjusting to the vast changes brought about by one governmental decision.

"Ford Motor Company was building huge gas-guzzling automobiles in 1979, nearly ten years after the first fuel crisis hit us. In one year, Ford lost over a billion dollars.

"External change," he continued, "is accelerating and compounding at an incredible rate.

"Alvin Toffler has commented that the human race as we know it has been around for eight hundred lifetimes. Only one hundred and fifty of those lifetimes have been spent out of caves. The printed word is not much older than eight lifetimes. Perhaps as many as half the inventions people created during those eight hundred lifetimes have taken place in the last two. This is because we could accumulate and profit from knowledge and technology more easily than ever before.

"Forty years ago, J. Robert Oppenheimer, the 'Father of the Atomic Bomb,' wrote:

> *One thing that is new is the prevalence of newness. The changing scale and scope of change itself. So that the world alters as we walk on it. So that the years of a man's life measure not some small growth or rearrangement or moderation of what he learned in childhood, but a great upheaval.*

"Thirty years ago a man named Warren Bennis wrote, 'Change has now become a permanent and accelerating factor in American life.'"

Brian said, "One of the results of the acceleration of change is that two of your beneficiary groups are changing rapidly. Your guest market is undergoing a revolution of rising expectations that will be impossible to satisfy using traditional methods. The labor force is also changing. For example, most of your grandparents worked in one job all their lives. Now, the average person changes jobs more than five times during his or her career. Even when a person stays in the same job, the skills required are constantly changing. Yield management, call accounting, and point-of-sale equipment with remote printers, have all come into existence in the last eight years."

Brian paused, looking around the room. "I'd like to talk now about the ramifications of change for management.

"Nearly ten years ago two very astute observers of business, Anthony Athos and Richard Tanner Pascal, wrote the following."

Brian put on his glasses and picked up a well-worn book from the table and read:

> *As we review our stock of business innovation in the period of dramatic change since World War II, we observe a troubling disparity. While our technological advances have been tremendous and our formation of capital enormous, Western organizations run themselves in 1981 in much the same way as in 1940. There is still a troublesome tension between boss and subordinate.... We still esteem the tough, individualistic and dominating U.S. leadership ideal that prevailed in past centuries.... To be sure, changes have taken place. New attitudes in society at large have somewhat rounded the edges of traditional authority and command.... But our view is that contemporary values and beliefs about how to run organizations are remarkably similar to those of fifty years ago. Our world has changed, our society has changed, but our assumptions about management have ominously stayed much the same.*

"The results of this have been devastating," Brian said.

"First, American, English, and Canadian productivity has declined in relation to the rest of the world.

"Second, to provide adequate motivation, organizations have become incredibly bureaucratic. General Motors used to have seventy-two levels between the floor worker and the chairman. In your hotel, you have a labor force of about one person per room. But almost a quarter of your employees are involved in supervising and checking up on the other three quarters.

"As you know, the concept of scientific management was developed by Frederick Taylor in the early part of this century. Taylor advocated a scientific study of how jobs were performed in order to organize those jobs so that they were performed in the most efficient manner. He determined how many coals could fit in a shovel and how many shovelfuls of coal a person could reasonably shovel in a day and this became the quota for a job. The entire set of rewards and punishments was established around these quotas. If he met the quotas, a worker and his or her boss were rewarded. If they didn't, they were punished. If a boss wanted to get ahead, they would exceed quotas. In other words, you could be a star in the organization if you got your workers to do more than they could reasonably be expected to accomplish.

"Think about the implications of this theory," Brian said.

"Many managers interpreted Taylor to mean that people — except for you and me, and I am not sure about you — are basically lazy. They do as little as possible. They will lie, cheat and steal if they can get away with it. Therefore, how do you get them to behave in a way they don't want to? What will motivate them to be good?"

"Fear. Watching them every moment," said John Wolcott. This was his first comment. No one seemed sure whether he was stating his own philosophy or not.

"Right. Now look at what has happened using the traditional management methods."

"What about theory Y and theory Z, which assume a different way of motivating people?" asked Bill.

"I agree with you that these theories are a sign of progress," Brian said. "These represent more realistic assumptions about what motivates the worker. Studies have shown, for example, that the ability to adjust the management style from individual to individual is much more effective. So at least we have progressed in theories of motivation to the idea that people are different, and even the individual varies from one day to the next.

"We still are hung up on the idea, however, that motivation is what one person gives to another. We spend vast amounts of time and money trying to change attitudes. We follow the underlying assumption that there is something basically wrong with the attitudes of normal people, and the solution is to get them to be more exceptional, like we are.

"I feel," Brian said, "that people basically want to do a good job once their basic needs are met. What motivates them more than anything else is the chance to be successful. The work itself can be a motivator. It is for me and it is for you."

Brian then showed a tape of Dr. W. Edwards Deming discussing his fourteen points. He handed out a reprinted page from Mary Walton's classic book *The Deming Management Method*. There was a lively discussion about the 14 points and the group generally concurred with them.

After a short break, Brian began again. He drew a triangle on the flipchart and discussed some of the difficulties of the traditional organization chart. "If management is at the top of the chart," he pointed out, "the guests are at the bottom, separated from the top by six layers. If you wanted to give a suggestion to Lorna, you wouldn't give it to a room attendant because the message might never arrive.

"A second problem with the chart," he pointed out, "is that it compartmentalizes rather than lateralizes.

"Let me give you an example," he said, noticing the bewildered expressions in his audience.

"Let's say you have a fry cook named Willy and a breakfast food server named George. Willy, in the eyes of George, never gets it right. His orders are slow in coming out, he puts too much grease on the eggs, he overcooks over-easy eggs, and his bacon tastes rancid.

"In the eyes of Willy, George is sullen, unfriendly, always forgets to put his orders in on time, he's always in a big hurry and Willy, if he weren't such a good Christian, would probably do everything he could to delay the orders going out to George.

"Willy is very upset about the bacon. Secretly, he agrees with George that the bacon is rancid.

"That brings in Mildred, the receiving clerk. Mildred is the one who accepts the rancid bacon at the loading dock. Because the chef likes to keep his inventory as low as possible, Mildred can't reject rancid bacon even if she knew for sure what it looked like, which she doesn't.

"Ah, and this brings in Ben. Ben owns ABC Provisions, a meat purveyor. He works eighty hours a week and sometimes drives his own truck. Ben can never count on the orders from the hotel, so when he gets an order for bacon in the morning it's usually a surprise to him. So, he picks up bacon wherever he can.

"Now, George answers to whom?"

"The hostess," said Walter.

"And who does the hostess answer to?"

"The dining room manager."

"And who does the dining room manager answer to?"

"Me, the food and beverage director."

"Good. And Willy, who does he answer to?" asked Brian.

"The sous chef," said Andy.

"And who does the sous chef answer to?"

"Me, the executive chef," said Andy.

"And Mildred, who does she answer to?" asked Brian.

"The purchasing manager," said Sam.

"And who does he answer to?"

"The controller."

"Now the key question. When was the last time Ben, Mildred, Willy and George met together to discuss their common problems?"

"Never," said Bill.

"The chain of command," Brian said pointing at the triangle, "defeats them. If anything, they end up hating each other. And why do they hate each other? George and Willy particularly hate each other. Is it because one is lazy, dishonest, a liar and cheater? Is the answer a motivational training program for George? Will that bring better bacon to the guest? Is the answer to fire Ben? What about withholding Mildred's pay raise? Will that bring better bacon to the guest?"

Brian answered his own question. "No. They hate each other because each one wants to do their job well and each one feels that the other one is preventing him or her from doing his or her job well.

"The standard chain of command compartmentalizes people vertically, while their work is conducted laterally. Services flow back and forth along the bottom of the triangle rather than top down. You can turn the chain of command on its side, turn it all the way over, put the guest on the top. But you won't effect the slightest bit of change in the real problem, which is that the structure itself defeats success. It limits communication, it puts too much distance between the guest and the senior management, and it prevents people from successfully serving their guests in a consistent fashion. In my opinion, this chain of command alone may prevent you from realizing your potential.

"I'd like to introduce to you a different concept."

Brian looked at Lorna. "What would you do if you got lots of complaints about breakfast service?"

"I guess I'd put the heat on the food and beverage director," Lorna said.

"And what would you do, Walter?"

"That's obvious, I'd put the heat on the dining room manager," said Walter, smiling.

"And," Brian said, "a smart dining room manager would try to make some changes so that the heat would come off her, something which is short-term in nature. She will put the heat on George. His morale continues to decline and, if anything, the service gets worse."

"What if you have seven 'Georges' working in your coffee shop?" asked Walter.

There was general laughter.

"Hire Dr. Deming," said Sam.

Brian joined the laughter.

"Dr. Deming would look at the system," Brian said, "and he would try to figure out statistically how bad the problem really is. He would figure out a way of talking with the customers and determining what their preconceptions were, what their needs were and whether their needs were being met. He would analyze the system under which the employees were working, and he would find ways to get Willy, Mildred, and Ben together."

"Hold everything," said Walter. "Maybe I could get Willy and George together. That's my job. But Sam's not going to let Mildred get involved, and none of us have any control over Ben."

"Is that true?" Brian asked, looking at Sam.

Sam looked uncomfortably at the ceiling. "I guess if I were there, it would be all right."

"Ah, now I know what Sam means," Brian teased Sam. "You want to control them."

"Not exactly," Sam protested. "But Mildred does not really understand how things work. She might either fight the other two people or give in to them. She can't really make that kind of decision. Even the purchasing agent has to check with the food and beverage director and the chef. Otherwise they wouldn't get the right kind of quality. And I'm not sure Mildred would know the quality that the chef wants."

"Why don't they?" asked Brian, pushing his point.

"Lack of training," interjected Bill.

"There's no time," said Walter, lamely. "The chef is practically burnt-out as it is. He certainly doesn't have time to train the purchasing agent and the stock room clerk."

"Not enough time because of what?" asked Fred.

"Because he's doing the stockroom clerks' job for them," Lorna said.

"Let's take a break," Brian said. The exchange was in danger of pushing a little further than he wanted, and he didn't want any member of the executive committee to have to dig in their heels and defend a position against the boss.

He knew that Walter and Sam needed time to think through what was being presented.

Not to his surprise, Walter and Sam left the room together deep in discussion.

Lorna noticed that Brian was religiously taking a break on the hour. She walked outside, resisting the urge to call the regional office. They were only vaguely aware of the retreat, and she doubted that they would approve if they were aware.

She was sure something would go wrong at the hotel in their absence and she would get some grief. She hoped the fact that it was a weekend in the fall meant that her superiors were also away, hopefully not in Vermont.

Lorna recognized that although the regional office might approve by default a corporate retreat, they would have no trouble laying the blame if something went wrong.

After the break, Brian continued. "If Dr. Deming is right, people are already motivated, they already want to do a good job, to be successful.

"They can be doing their very best, however, and the system can defeat them."

He turned over a flip chart sheet. "If he is right, once they can meet their basic family needs, people are motivated by the following:

- **Knowing what is expected**
- **Responsibility**
- **Working with a team**

- **Sharing ideas**
- **Recognition**
- **Being trusted**
- **Success**
- **Security**
- **Having the authority to carry out their job**
- **Control over outcomes**

"Notice that these are similar to what your staff said motivated them. Maybe at the time of Frederick Taylor, the suspicion that workers felt toward bosses was so ingrained, and the mistrust that bosses felt toward workers was so deeply entrenched, that there was no other way of motivating than by fear. However, even then, fear was not a really good motivator. It only ensured that people didn't have much enjoyment or sense of satisfaction from their jobs, except in terms of what the jobs were able to provide for their families.

"Today, we need to structure jobs to provide more of *these* motivational factors," he said, referring back to the list.

"Now," Brian continued, "let's talk about reporting relationships. American management theory holds that one person can effectively manage ten people. This is the concept of span of control. The critical word is 'control.' Traditional thinking holds that the job of the manager is to control those people below them in the hierarchy.

"A more effective view holds that the job of the manager is to provide the environment that meets the employees' needs, while at the same time making sure that the work unit meets the organization's customers' needs.

"The manager's job is to lead, not control. His or her job is to help the staff improve the services and products of the department, to back up the staff when they exercise their authority, to train and to solve problems."

Brian concluded his point.

"Who is running the hotel today?" he asked.

"The front office manager," Lorna said.

"What is your occupancy?"

"Seventy-five percent," she said.

"How do you know he will do a good job?"

"He's been around, and I've worked with him for six years in other hotels," said Joan.

"You trust him?" Brian asked.

"Yes. He'll know what to do when unpredictable things happen," Joan answered.

"Will he be able to handle them?"

"If he values his job," said the engineer, laughing.

"What's the difference between him and his assistant?" asked Brian.

"His assistant is not a known quantity," said Fred, "and she comes from Marriott. She would probably try to run the hotel like a Marriott."

Brian ignored the comment and concluded.

"Planning, controlling, and directing, which are traditional management functions, are all jobs that the workers can share in if they have the knowledge, if they understand the organization and its purpose. The more the assistant knows, the more she will be able to function on her own. This requires training and authority."

"And risk," said John.

"And risk."

chapter
XIII

the Chain of Service

They had a spirited and light-hearted conversation over a delicious lunch prepared by the owner of the inn, a retired New York advertising executive and gourmet chef. It seemed to Lorna that the group was more relaxed and open with each other than they had ever been before. There was no doubt that being away from the hotel in a beautiful setting made a difference. But it was also important to have someone like Brian, who understood their situation and who had broad experience, to talk with them. He was an irreverent maverick, but he was not irresponsible. He had a good mind and wonderful ideas, while his ego was not tied up in his point of view. His whole lecture style was conversational. He listened as much as he talked. Somehow, the strength he felt in his convictions gave the entire group more self-confidence to face a risky and uncertain future.

"Last spring," Brian began the afternoon session, "I visited a factory in Shanghai, China, that uses a system that they called TQ, or Total Quality. Although many factories in China experience difficulty, this factory was extremely well run, producing cotton fabric that was sold to 100 countries worldwide. The fabric had to exceed the standards of the most stringent of all these countries and did so with ease consistently, year after year.

"I asked the manager what he does during the day. He said every day his routine is pretty much the same. In the morning he walks the factory, observing the workers, talking with them, trying to determine what their particular needs are, and reviewing the statistical charts that are located on the walls throughout the factory. In the afternoon he meets with the engineers. Sometimes he also meets with the production people. Sometimes he meets with marketing or with visitors from other countries who are buying the materials from the factory. He is very available, even though there are over thirty workers in his factory for every supervisor or manager.

"I found it very interesting to note the things he doesn't do. He doesn't spend a great deal of time writing or reading memos. He spends virtually no time disciplining subordinates. He spends relatively little time on the budgeting and financial review process. Because the factory is under statistical control, and finances are also under statistical control, he looks only at exceptional financial numbers. Finally, he spends very little time in what we would call crisis management."

Brian continued, "Before some Japanese engineers installed the Total Quality program, the manager said he spent most of his time solving problems. Machinery was constantly breaking down, workers were unhappy and required continuous discipline. Supervisors often sided openly with the workers against management. No one wanted to become a supervisor despite the increase in pay. The product of the factory at that time was very poor, so he had to also spend a great deal of time working with unhappy customers and reworking projects that came in. Needless to say, the factory was not profitable. Thus, before the Total Quality system came into his factory, he was spending most of his time doing the jobs of his subordinates, of the quality control people, and of the marketing people. Consequently, he had relatively little time to think about and to prepare for the future.

"Before, he had spent a great deal of time trying to control his subordinates. Now the entire factory is totally under control, not by management, however, but by a system.

"Before, he had had to mediate between departments competing for scarce resources. Now resources are allocated in a cooperative manner, as the system dictates. And there are more resources because resources are better used. The cost of production has actually declined as the quality has increased.

"This afternoon, I would like to share with you how this Total Quality system works and how you can put it to work for you.

"In its essence, total quality in manufacturing is a five-step system.

"First, determine what the customer wants now and will want in the future.

"Second, measure the quality of the product.

"Third, work upstream in the manufacturing process and measure the quality of each subcomponent of the final product.

"Fourth, involve everyone in improving the quality — commit all resources to quality.

"Fifth, create the best possible work environment for the staff.

"In this country, as you know, there is a crisis in the quality of our products. Our enormous national debt is a direct measurement of the poor quality of the goods we manufacture.

"A few years ago it was estimated that twenty-five percent of what we manufacture is unusable. It must be reworked, scrapped, or sold at a discount. If this estimate is accurate, this means that the products we manufacture cost twenty-five percent more than they need to.

"Nor is the problem limited to manufacturing. Karl Albrecht, in his book *At America's Service*, estimates that as much as forty percent of our services don't meet the needs of the consumer. For example, a study conducted a few years ago showed that seventy-five percent of hospital bills contain inaccuracies.

"Many CEOs of service businesses are alarmed that while consumers' demands are escalating, the ability to meet these demands is severely hampered by the cost and availability of labor. This is particularly true in the luxury end of the hotel business. When management seeks to improve quality, the traditional approach is to try to squeeze more productivity and consistency out of the staff, without addressing the systems in which the staff works. We are rapidly reaching the upper limits of the traditional system's capabilities.

"In the example I gave this morning — George, Willy, Mildred, and Ben — you can see the limits of the existing system. The Total Quality system I described works in manufacturing. It helped Ford to go from a one billion dollar loss one year to more than two billion dollars in profits a few years later. Right now, Ford cannot make enough cars to fill its demand. And Ford is just one example of how the Total Quality system works in America. Another example is that American-built Hondas are of identical quality to Japanese-built Hondas, and they are built just as efficiently."

John raised his hand. "I have been reading about the Quality Movement in manufacturing and I know it works there. How can we apply the same concepts to the service industries, particularly a hotel?" he asked.

"The translation is going to be difficult," Brian said. "It's no wonder that service organizations have been slow to adapt a more effective system of management, even in Japan. This, in spite of the fact that the service business is a major growth industry worldwide.

"There are several reasons why the translation is so difficult. First, the way the service is delivered is as important as the service itself. Perceptions of good service in a restaurant are affected by many attributes, including the friendliness and responsiveness of the staff, as well as the quality of the food.

"Second," he continued, "a large percentage of the staff deal directly with the paying customer. Any one person can destroy perceptions of service. This gives a hotel a high degree of vulnerability.

"Third is the complexity and unpredictability of demand, particularly in hotels, hospitals, and restaurants.

"In manufacturing, prediction of demand is a key factor for success because it enables you to control resources. Lack of predictability is a problem you want to avoid. In the service industry, lack of predictability is a fact of life. You don't know, for example, what a guest is going to order for breakfast, or exactly when they are going to show up, or even if they are going to show up at all. Sometimes the guests don't know these things in advance.

"You have to be like the fire department, sitting around with a lot of expensive equipment and manpower for a fire that may not occur. You have to be continuously alert for as many eventualities as possible."

He paused, several heads nodded. "There are several things that service organizations can do to eliminate unpredictability. A fast food franchise, for example, will limit the menu items they serve. They develop systems to manufacture hamburgers before the customer arrives. They limit eventualities and control predictability by controlling their customers.

"Another thing that companies can do is to conduct extensive market research to be able to predict more carefully what their customers are going to want. Marriott spends an enormous amount each year trying to predict what customers will want, trying to anticipate trends, and at the same time, trying to reduce the number of eventualities.

"Marriott builds specific products for specific market segments. Some of their hotels don't have restaurants at all. Some are for elderly people, some are for long-term corporate guests. Each of these strategies reduces the number of eventualities that management faces. It adds predictability and controls waste.

"Why not follow a similar strategy in your hotel?" asked Brian.

"Flexibility is part of our product," Lorna said. "Our target market wants the maximum flexibility. They want to be whimsical. They are also successful because of their ability to respond quickly to change, to make last minute decisions. They may want to fly out of New York for a quick meeting to solve an unanticipated problem and have us delay another meeting scheduled in the hotels. Or keep their bags ready to be unpacked for them.

"Or they might arrive jetlagged from Tokyo and need to send a telex at three in the morning," added Sarah. "Their success is due to their rapid response to changing conditions. And we have to be able to follow their lead, to dance with them even if the tune changes, or if they go from a foxtrot to a waltz."

"It seems to me," Brian concluded, "that the ability to respond to all eventualities puts a great burden on a luxury hotel's management. To maintain high quality, hotel management has a tendency to get involved in those transactions that take the staff of the hotel away from their routine. Management then tries to have the staff obey the rules and perform routine jobs as much as possible. Given the traditional mistrust between management and staff, the former has a tough time delegating flexibility to the latter. A change would enable the line staff to have the authority to respond to both the routine requests and special requests of their guests. Ideally, they would see the situation through your eyes, respond as you would respond and take chances as you would. When that happens, you stop fighting fires."

There was a long pause while that sunk in.

"This will take a great deal of training," said Bill.

"And risk-taking on our part," said Joan quietly.

"The final difference between manufacturing and a luxury hotel," Brian said, "is the number of service outlets and job categories. A hotel guest purchases many different services from many different departments. These departments are the internal customers of other departments in the back of the house. There is no single production line. There are multiple lines that are interconnected. Improving services in one area may actually harm another area.

"For example," he continued, "when I talked to the storeroom people, it was clear that maintaining an accurate inventory was extremely important to their success. What do you think they recommend to help them be more successful?"

"Close the storeroom except during their working hours," said Walter.

"Great idea," said Sam, laughing.

"What's wrong with their idea?" asked Brian.

"The chef would not be able to enjoy success in his job," Lorna said.

"So, it sounds like one department's success could guarantee failure for another person or department. This is what I meant the other day when I said that too many of your systems are established for the convenience of one group.

"Clearly there is a built-in conflict between this department and their customers. And there are a number of other built-in conflicts. Give me some examples of where one department's success could be another department's failure," Brian said.

"Preventative maintenance on the kitchen equipment during the working hours of the maintenance department," said Chet.

"Rooming guests in rooms that are not made up," said Joan. "This gets them out of the lobby but creates a problem for housekeeping."

"Eliminating overtime creates good numbers for the accounting department but may harm the service to the guests," said Sam.

"I never thought I would hear you say that," said Fred.

"So, just removing the barriers to success department by department would tend to create systems that are self-serving," Brian said. "In fact, removing barriers in one department might create barriers for another."

Brian paused.

"Thus," he said, "to improve quality throughout an organization, we need a unifying process that links the various departments in a common purpose. I call this process 'The Chain of Service.'"

Brian turned the next page on the flip chart.

"The whole chain is driven by the guest — the paying customer. George, the waiter, must respond to his customers' needs. George is Willy's customer so Willy must respond to George's needs. Mildred serves Willy's needs and Ben serves Mildred's needs.

"Each link in the chain adds value to the next link, the customer. If the link does not add value to the process of production, it simply shouldn't be there. To improve the quality of services, there must be information from the customers and constant innovation to improve the process of production.

"The rest of the afternoon we will discuss these two processes — finding out what the customer wants and figuring out better ways of providing it."

After a short break, Brian began a dialogue with the group that lasted into the early evening. Some samples of the discussion:

"What is our overall purpose?" asked Brian.

"Create the best hotel in New York City," said Ruth.

"For whom?"

"For our target market."

"How would you describe the target market?"

"Wealthy, not concerned about cost."

"But wants value."

"Loyal."

"An individual as opposed to a group."

"Fussy."

"Gourmet."

"Long stays."

"Frequent stays."

"So, you want this customer to be totally satisfied with the service of the hotel at all times?" asked Brian.

"Perfect service," Lorna said.

"Sure, sure, Lorna. We are talking about the real world. I would settle for eighty percent satisfaction."

"No," Lorna said. "*Perfect service.* That is our job. *Perfect service.* Perfect service will bring us the best hotel in New York. We already have the building — if John will fix it up — and the location."

Even Brian was awed by the forcefulness of Lorna's statement. The rest of the group was speechless — and more than a little nervous.

"Lorna, we simply cannot provide perfect service to all people at all times. It's a mathematical impossibility," said Chet.

"Yes, we can, and we will. That's what I thought you committed to."

"But how? Nobody in New York provides perfect service."

"How should I know? If I knew, I would have done it already. But we are going to figure it out.

"This morning," she continued, "it came to me that perfect service is simply a matter of meeting our guests' needs all the time. Their needs are really what they perceive to be their needs at the moment."

"Perceptions are reality."

"Right," Lorna said. "In thinking about this, I realized that what we need to do is to find out what those perceived needs are and continuously find out how we are doing in meeting them, just like Brian said.

"In other words," she paused, looking around the room, "we need to find out what the perceptions are and mobilize the entire hotel to create those perceptions. Perfect service is when the guests feel that we have perfect service. No matter how hard we try, if our ideal guest does not perceive perfect service, then we have failed."

There was a lot of initial resistance to the idea of perfect service. However, Brian noticed that the term "perfect service" began creeping into the dialogue with increasing frequency, as if each person wanted to savor it.

"How are you going to measure these perceptions so that you are getting continuous feedback?" he asked.

Before they could answer, he said, "Really effective manufacturing organizations create products that their customers perceive as meeting their needs. The companies spent a great deal of time and money measuring what those perceptions are. In other words, they collect market data."

"We can do the same thing. We can create a profile of our target customer. This will help determine what he or she needs," said Sarah.

"That will take time. How can we get a better fix on the market while you're doing the profile?"

"How do we measure it now?" asked John.

"Guest comment cards."

"Focus groups, once in awhile."

"Individual interviews."

"Letters of complaint."

"Feedback from the front office staff."

"The Palmer Happy Guest Index, the infamous HGI."

"Are you completely satisfied with the results of this way of gathering information?" asked Brian.

"Not enough people get the information."

"No, as you pointed out, it's slow."

"Not enough customers interviewed."

"I propose," Brian said, "that we develop a system together in which we get feedback from at least half of all guests. And then we ask them all the same questions so that our statistical methods are consistent. How could we do this? One way is to use our staff. We should develop a statistically valid questionnaire and train some of the hotel's staff in how to conduct interviews. We should find time in which guests will not be inconvenienced by the interview."

"That sounds like a lot of work."

"Perhaps," Brian said, "but it should give us information none of your competition has. Also, we have all seen studies that show that guests who complain and get a response are more likely to return than guests who are unhappy but don't complain. With this system, we are giving them a chance to complain. By just listening to them we can express our recognition of them."

After some discussion, Lorna said, "Brian, why don't you work with Sarah and develop a questionnaire that makes sense and we can try it out as quickly as possible. Both of you could train the interviewers."

"Will do," Brian said, making a note.

Joan said, "I'd like to have several people trained to do the interviews from reservations, telephone and front desk. This would give us flexibility. And for telephones and reservations, it would give them a chance to get out and greet the guests."

Lorna asked, "What would be the best time to interview guests?"

"In the checkout line. Also at the checkout desk. One person could process their voucher while another is conducting the interview."

Lorna said, "I would like to begin the interview process within two weeks. Is that feasible?"

Everyone agreed, although a little reluctantly.

Sarah said, "I suggest that we interview only our target market."

When they had agreed upon the details, Brian presented a short lecture on the statistical process with the promise of more training when he gave them the "Service Innovation" course.

He reminded them that finding out what the end user, the paying guest, needed was only part of the equation. They would also need to find out what each customer in the chain of service needed from those who served them.

chapter XIV
Innovation

The afternoon opened with a team-building exercise. The group performed an exercise first as individuals and then as members of a team. The team performance was much higher than the highest individual score.

Brian's voice penetrated through the animated discussions.

"Let's analyze how decisions made as individuals compare with decisions made as a group."

As the group members worked through this analysis, they began to see that decisions made by the group were better, more innovative and more courageous than individual choices.

"Now, I would like to show you how this applies to the task of constantly improving quality that we've set ourselves to."

During the rest of the afternoon, Brian led the group through a discussion on the innovation process as it applied to the hotel.

"A strategy for constantly improving quality," he said, "will not work without constantly innovating. This innovation traditionally has been the prerogative of a chosen few people — the manager, the owner, and the few people who advise them. What we have seen with this exercise is that well-run groups innovate better than individuals. Almost inevitably, the group's score is better than the leader's individual score. Therefore, the most productive activity a skilled leader can perform is to involve subordinates and others in the innovative process. We know this for a fact, and yet the average employee in your hotel feels that his or her ideas are not being sought out by management. In fact, you meet employees on the average of only once a month."

"If you asked the staff to take over management of the hotel, you would have chaos," said Walter.

"Didn't we have this discussion before?" asked Brian patiently. "The employees will not take over the leadership of the hotel. That leadership is up to you. The employees won't take over the major decision-making, that also is up to you, within, of course, the guidelines put down by Palmer and the owners.

"After a thorough measurement system is in place, you might find, for example, that the most important attribute for the coffee shop at breakfast is speed of service. If the customers indicate that speed needs improvement, then this should be the topic of discussion for the breakfast wait staff.

"All available wait staff should meet once a week to review customer feedback and work on the problem. Because the problem involves the kitchen, the breakfast kitchen should join the group."

Brian described a three-step process that he felt should be followed in problem solving.

He wrote the following on the flip chart:

PROBLEM SOLVING:

1. **Analyze** — determine the gap and why there is a gap.

    a. **What's the ideal condition?**

    b. **What's reality?**

    c. **What causes the difference?**

"This may take some research," he said. "It's critical to study when and under what conditions a problem occurs. Does it occur everyday? Does it occur when the hotel is full? How often does it occur?

"Once you have determined exactly *what* the problem is, try to analyze *why* the problem exists and what the probable causes are.

"This also may take study. The employees should be involved in the analysis of the gap."

He wrote again:

  2. Plan — develop solutions

     a. Quick fix

     b. Long-term strategies

     c. Analysis of cost and return

"Sometimes these solutions can be implemented very quickly. Sometimes the solutions take much longer. Many solutions should to be presented to management. Staff themselves can help prepare the presentations, costing out equipment purchases, for example."

There was considerable discussion about each point, but surprisingly little resistance.

Brian returned to the flip chart.

  3. Act

     a. Implement

     b. Evaluate

     c. Repeat process

"Each of these steps should involve all employees in a given department, not just a small group. It will mean sharing information with them so that they can help you make intelligent decisions."

Lorna stood up to close the meeting for the day. "I am very excited about this concept," she began. "It's going to be very difficult to implement and very time-consuming. What it will mean, among other things, is that we will have to really figure out and write down our service standards and job procedures as soon as possible. And we may have to turn around six months later and write them again based on feedback from our customers. We are also going to need to retrain our staff to make sure they know their jobs."

"I guess there is no such thing as a free lunch," said Sam.

She led a round of applause for Brian.

chapter XV

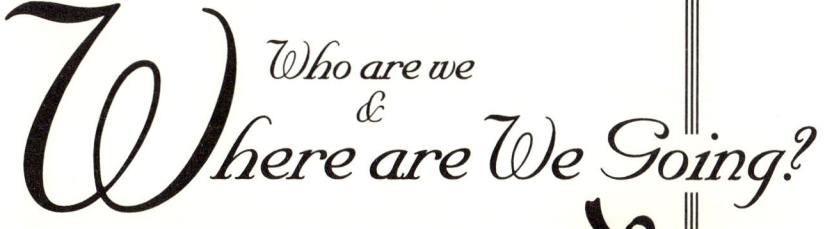

Who are we & Where are We Going?

The next morning the group struggled through a definition of their mission for an hour and produced a very brief statement:

> *The Palmer Madison Avenue exists to provide constantly improving services to its guests.*

Brian personally felt it was a sort of vanilla mission statement, not very exciting, but adequate. It was theirs, however, and John seemed happy.

"Now," Brian said, "I suggest you develop some basic rules for behavior which can guide you and the staff — guiding principles."

Again, he asked them to choose words or phrases. He wrote their ideas on the flip chart.

- **Trust**
- **Skills**

- **Select the best**
- **Total flexibility**
- **Innovation — anticipate needs**

He divided the group into teams to work on statements describing each guiding principle.

John and Lorna sat on the inn's porch and worked on the principle of "trust."

After some time, they had drafted a statement.

> *Our customers — that is, our owners, our guests, our staff, Palmer hotels, and our community — will always be treated with trust. We assume that if our staff is given the proper amount of information, they can be counted upon to act in the best interest of the organization. Therefore, they must be constantly informed. Staff will be given the full authority needed to carry out their jobs. Managers may make decisions within the limits of their departmental budgets. It is assumed that these decisions will be made to assure the long-term viability of the business.*

"John," asked Lorna, "what if this means that an employee of the dining room should give away a meal, if the guest is unhappy?"

"Why not?"

"John, they would give away the store and it's your family's store."

"Sometimes I get carried away with ideas and get in trouble for them," he said, "but let's think about why they would give away the store. They work in the store and only if they have been hurt by the store would they be so foolish as to let emotions override reason."

"I'm afraid they have been hurt. They have seen managers come and go. They have felt powerless except for the union. They have offered suggestions that were ignored. Even I have turned down ideas that were good," confessed Lorna.

"Why?"

"As we discuss all of this, I think it is because either I felt that they would want more and more, and not respect management, or I felt that the regional office would think that I was being a weak manager. All my career, I have gotten ahead when I was tough and fallen back when I was considered weak. To be frank with you, John, it is doubly tough to be a woman because men in senior positions are always looking for frailties. If you lose your cool, you are accused of being hysterical or even a bitch. How many screaming male chefs do you hear being called hysterical or bitches?"

John laughed. "Going back to the staff. Do you think all the hurt they have felt in the past can be overcome, Lorna?"

"I don't know," she said.

"Has your own attitude toward Palmer Hotels changed this weekend?" he asked.

"A great deal," Lorna said.

"How?" he persisted.

"John, if this gets back to them, I'm dead."

John laughed and pointed to the guiding principle on trust.

Lorna felt her face flush. "OK, we are in it together." She paused. "What I have discovered is that I resent not being trusted myself, that I resent having all these people giving me free advice and then double-checking everything I do. I resent all these reports, most of which are either not read or are used as a hammer to hit me over the head. I guess I also resent the fact that there is no easy access to corporate. They never ask for my ideas and they never spend time with me as a consultant, helping me figure out the solutions to my own problems."

She continued. "In the last few weeks, I have begun to realize how wasteful it all is and how foolish it must appear, even to the pot washer in the kitchen.

"Another thing that bothers me is that there is tremendous emphasis on how your hotel is doing as compared to everyone else, not just the Marriott down the street but to other Palmer hotels. We end up competing with each other, and we do the same thing internally so that there is always a battle for resources. So that nobody trusts anyone else."

"Lorna, let me ask you something. Do you have enough confidence in Palmer and CTX to feel that they can change toward a more effective style of management?"

"I am not sure. You're saying that I have to trust them to come around to a different style of management."

"Yes."

"This is so strange coming from an owner."

"Lorna, I need Palmer. They generate a lot of room nights for us. More important, however, they generate consistency. I feel that they can and will gradually change. Some of their divisions have already changed radically. And I think CTX certainly wants to be more successful than it is now. What we are talking about is a strategy and a system for success. If we can prove success, they will listen. Lorna, as you really get into these changes, I predict you will have much more confidence in the ability of CTX and Palmer Hotels to change. Trust of others comes from confidence and trust in yourself."

Lorna looked at him for a long time.

"Where did you get all this stuff?" she asked.

"From the silver spoon they found in my mouth at birth. And from a thirty-year process of trying to reconcile myself with my parents. Fortunately, I had lots of help from people who could explain things to me and help me understand them better myself."

"Are you saying that organizations are like families?"

"Yes," he said. "Just like families work things out, so must organizations. After all, the family is an organization. Organizations got bigger than families because families couldn't survive alone."

At this moment, Brian reconvened the group, and each team presented its principles. Some were very brief, some were a little too wordy. All of them seemed to be very elegant to Lorna.

She and John presented theirs to the group last.

"Does that mean that a maintenance person can make a room change?" asked Joan.

"Yes," Lorna said. "Why not?"

There was a pause.

Chet said, "Why not? They know whether the faucet can be fixed or not — or at least they should. They could just pick up the phone in front of the guest and move the guest to an available room."

"What if there are no available rooms?"

"Why don't we simply never sell out?" asked Sarah.

"Yes, why don't we keep fifteen rooms out of circulation. Ninety-percent occupancy is about as high as we can run without creating major problems anyway."

The group looked at John.

"What's the best way to protect my family's investment over the long run?" he asked.

"Never sell out." There was a chorus of agreement.

"I guess I have to trust you," he said to general laughter.

chapter
XVI

Driving Force

After another delicious lunch, Brian opened the Sunday afternoon session with a brief talk about strategy.

"Up to now," he began, "we have discussed styles of leadership and systems for improving quality on a never-ending basis. We have developed a mission statement and some general rules for our process of transformation.

"You have also made a couple of strategic decisions. Can you give me an example?"

"To bring John with us."

"Sell our ideas to Marriott."

Brian waited patiently as several more lighthearted comments were thrown out.

"Never sell out," Sarah said.

"That's a guiding principle."

"No, she means never sell all the rooms in inventory."

"Right," Brian said. "That's a strategy."

"What I suggest we do this afternoon is develop a few more strategies."

"What is a strategy? One person, Benjamin Tregoe, in his book *Top Management Strategy*, defines it as a framework to guide those choices that determine the nature and direction of an organization.

"The problem the organizations I work with often have is not a lack of strategies but a lack of commitment to one strategic direction. They jump around from one strategy to another like a fish out of water. Often different sections have different strategies.

"One of the most critical things for you to decide is your market strategy." He went to the flip chart and wrote:

- **What do we sell? — Product**

- **To whom do we sell it? — Market**

- **What return on investment? — Profit**

"It seems to me that these are the critical questions facing you. Which is the most important to you?" he asked.

There was some discussion about this. Initially, there was no clear agreement.

"I think we should determine the products and services at the very highest level and then figure out who we can sell them to," said Ruth.

"But doesn't that imply an assumption about who we are selling to?" asked Sarah.

"Let's start with return on investment and back into the product and the market," said Walter, eyeing John.

"How can you figure out your return if you don't know what you've got?" John asked.

The discussion went on for awhile, shedding less and less light on which direction to go.

Finally, the group began to turn on Brian.

"Brian, in all due respect, why do we have to choose one? They are all interlocked; each effects the other."

Brian answered, "I feel that an organization needs one driving force, a single thrust in its marketing strategy that will guide all the other decisions made. If you try to focus on both return on investment *and* pleasing your market, you are going to be in trouble because you will either vacillate or you will pit one person or department against another."

Fred said, "This is really the environment we have been living in for years. We end up with the controller pursuing an ROI strategy and sales pursuing a 'market' strategy and Walter pursuing a 'product' strategy."

"No wonder you have a constant tug of war," Brian said.

There was more discussion and general agreement. As they thought about what Brian said, they realized that each of them felt committed to different driving forces.

"Palmer represents something different to each person," said Ruth.

"That raises a very interesting point," said Chet. "What happens if we select one strategy and then find that we are in conflict with Palmer or CTX?"

Brian, without knowing it, made a very prophetic statement. "A lot of people think that CTX is a very ROI-driven company. There is nothing wrong with a unit choosing another driving force, but they are raising a lot of sail in a freshening breeze."

"Meaning what, old salt?"

"It is a risky strategy because it means that something else will come ahead of short-term profits. You could do a fabulous job and still not come within the framework of success of your parent company.

"I suggest the following," he continued. "We spend our final afternoon session doing three things....

"First, decide the driving force between product, market and profit.

"Second, review our key factors for success.

"And third, make a few more strategic decisions."

chapter
XVII

"Facilitator"

As he had promised to do, Brian backed away from active involvement and let the group work on its own. Lorna had discussed her role with Brian. She was to facilitate the group. What a pompous sounding word — facilitate — a good reason why the academic world never made any sense to the business world.

However, having watched him for two days, she could see the power of facilitation as a meeting style. Steiner had a very different method of running a meeting. He did not particularly like meetings and encouraged limited participation. Everything was shorthand. Meetings were something which you got out of the way in order to get on with the business of running a hotel. At best, it was a pep talk and a way of ensuring that everyone understood the order of the day. His meetings were daily fifteen-minute affairs in which he went around the room in a crisp, highly directed fashion.

    STEINER: Mr. Smith. (Steiner always addressed people formally and expected the same.)

SMITH: Nothing, sir.

STEINER: Mr. Johnson

JOHNSON: We are expecting three VIPs: Mr. Smyser from Amalgamated Insurance; Mr. Ludwig, the general manager of the Frankfurt Palmer, who will be having dinner at L'etoile with Mr. and Mrs. Steiner at 7:30 p.m.; and Miss Giovanna from New York, who is a personal friend of Mrs. Falworth. I have arranged that each will be picked up at Logan by the limousine.

STEINER: What have you arranged for the rooms, Miss Danforth?

DANFORTH: They will each be in tower suites with the deluxe amenity package and a small gift from Shreve Crump and Lowe with your note. They will have a deluxe flower arrangement. The rooms are ready if you would like to look at them.

STEINER: Let's go up right after the meeting, Mr. Johnson. Anything else?

Steiner ran that type of meeting extremely well. It moved fast and everyone had a chance to talk about urgent problems that might affect the guest experience.

Lorna always enjoyed the meetings. They were exciting, tight, forceful. Steiner was asserting his personal leadership, making lightning-like decisions. The daily briefing re-emphasized his leadership.

She felt uncomfortable when personalities and conflicts intruded. None of the deep animosity that some members of Steiner's staff felt for each other surfaced in his daily briefing — no one would dare.

However, the daily briefing never focused on problem solving, problem prevention, or long-term strategy. Department heads were expected to solve their own problems. "I don't want problems, I want solutions," said Steiner, who had no patience for people who brought up open-ended problems.

It would be unthinkable for Steiner to ask, "How do you think we can improve the speed of room service?" or have an open-ended discussion.

Brian presented a different style altogether. He encouraged the introduction of problems. There was no penalty for not knowing the solution. And he supported creative thinking. He seemed to want people to jump outside their own role.

She noticed Chet increasingly expressed ideas about personnel and Fred, instead of showing his traditional territorial attitude, was visibly warming up to his ideas.

"Meetings are like making love," Brian joked at one point. "Speed is not the criteria for success."

Lorna saw how each type of meeting had its place. The short, dynamic pep rally served one purpose. It focused the property and its management team on the day's events.

The problem-solving session was altogether different. Sometimes its inspirational value was limited, its results slow in coming, but it prevented problems and it improved the product and the systems that produced the product.

The styles of leadership had to be different in each meeting just as the purpose differed.

This is how she began to realize that she had been trying to combine the two different styles in her executive committee meeting, to the confusion and frustration of the participants. Unlike Steiner, she genuinely needed and valued guidance from her associates. She had never had his overwhelming confidence and natural leadership ability. Although she would never dare admit it, sometimes she felt unsure about her decisions.

Steiner would charge ahead. He sometimes made poor decisions but seemed to never have any regrets. He just simply remade the decision.

As Lorna watched Brian, she realized that her style probably created insecurity on the part of her subordinates. Sometimes she was tough and aggressive, allowing no discussion. Other times she tried to get everyone to agree and listened to interminable rambling discussions with apparently endless patience.

Brian let the group know what kind of meeting they were in all the time. He signaled the group when he wanted to teach them something, and he signaled them again when he wanted to discuss something, and yet again when he wanted them to make a decision.

The term "facilitator" to Lorna had always meant "airy fairy" — indecisive leadership — the very thing she liked the least in her own style.

Brian, however, was a very good facilitator. He was basically strong, confident and passionate about his work, and he lost none of that as he pushed the group to come to decisions.

"Guide the process, lead the process, Lorna," he said. "Groups really do think better than individuals if they are well-led. Start by assuming that you have no idea what the solution is."

Lorna began the discussion with some trepidation. She walked up to Brian's list and turned around to face the group. There was dead silence.

For some reason she felt a twinge of terror.

"OK ─────── (Pause) ─────── does anyone disagree with the idea that we should focus on *one* of these rather than trying to serve many masters?"

There was no response. Lorna realized that she had made a mistake in phrasing the question that way. Yes, they disagree?

"John, how do you feel about focusing on just one?"

"After lunch, I came in here and puzzled over that. I also thought about our family's portfolio of investments and realized that our driving force is different with every area we go into. This creates a lot of drama within us. For example, some people feel that we should invest only in socially responsible areas. Most agree, but then have a difficult time deciding what a socially responsible investment is. Just about every investment you can make has some ties to a corrupt dictatorship or pollutes the atmosphere or supports a war somewhere."

"And...?" asked Lorna.

"And I guess I think we should focus on one driving force but I'm darned if I know which one."

"How do the rest of you feel?"

There was general agreement.

"I must confess that I would feel happier if we did not have to confront this issue," said Chet. "We have all changed a lot in the past two days and we are thinking like a team. We are each going to have a different idea about our driving force. Maybe it doesn't really make that much difference. Why kill a good thing on some 'Mickey Mouse' issue?"

Lorna had wondered about the same thing. She looked over to get Brian's help. Somehow Brian had snuck out of the room! That rat, she thought, and tried to cover her consternation by continuing her glance around the table. As she got to John, she realized that he alone had understood her panic in that instant. He smiled at her in a supportive manner.

"Well, I think..." he paused, drawing the attention to himself.

Bless you John, thought Lorna. She suspected John didn't have any formed thoughts, but was drawing the heat from a potentially embarrassing situation.

"I think," John repeated, "we should take a chance. If anything, making a decision like this will draw us closer together and help us continue as the Green Mountain Group in the future."

Lorna pulled a chair over near the flipchart and sat down.

"So, let's not pussyfoot around. Let's get on with it," she said, fully reversed.

There was a long pause. Then three people spoke at once. The discussion continued unabated for nearly an hour. Lorna began formulating a very clear idea after awhile but didn't push it on the group.

"Facilitator, facilitator," she kept repeating in her mind.

She said very little. Only John, and Brian, who had snuck back in the room, said less. Both were listening intently to the discussion, taking occasional notes.

She found her role was primarily in drawing out shy people (whose numbers were rapidly diminishing).

"Andy, how do you feel about what Sarah just said?"

"Well, she has a good point...."

"Talk to her, not me!"

"Well, she...you have a good point, Sarah. I think...," and Andy would continue, usually bringing up a fresh point of view.

Occasionally Lorna found herself untangling the discussion or clarifying.

"Wait a minute. Maybe you're both right...," or, "Let me see if I understand what you're saying...."

"So, what's the decision?" she finally asked, when it seemed to her that the group was closing in on a concensus.

"Could I just ask a question of Brian? Brian, what would Mr. Marriott choose?"

"Call him and ask him. What do you think he would say?" Brian shot the question back.

"I would guess he would say the market — who we are going to sell it to?"

"I would agree," said Sarah. "They spend an enormous amount of money on market research."

"What about the Plaza?"

"Product, I would bet," said Ruth. There was general agreement that the owner seemed to be focusing on producing what he felt was the ultimate definition of quality.

"What about Inter-Continental?"

"The new owners paid so much, they may have to go for profit."

"So, what about us?" Lorna guided them back.

The discussion had narrowed to product and market.

One of the market advocates was Walter. Now he took a different tack.

"My thought, up until now, was that we would survey the market and determine what they need and build from there. I was particularly concerned that we would change the restaurant concept and find it wouldn't fly in New York like the restaurant in the Palmer Lagos Hotel that has a fireplace in it. I'm serious. Certainly the market didn't ask for a rural Austrian restaurant with a fireplace in a city where the average temperature is ninety-two degrees in the shade.

"I was talking to Brian about Dr. Deming's philosophy during a break," he continued, "and Deming said you need to both refine your existing product with your customers and build new products that your customers haven't asked for yet, like Edison with a light bulb.

"What if we shoot for a super high-quality product and then select a client base that will support the product. We can get feedback from that client base but our central focus will be product refinement. The risk is lowered because we are in New York and there are a lot of up-market customers," concluded Walter.

This short speech sold the group, including John.

Lorna put in one more question, "Everything I read says we should be customer-driven. Aren't we going to appear arrogant by saying we are product-driven?"

Brian finally spoke, "How many companies that say they are customer-driven really are? Not many, I would guess. Maybe a law firm or an accounting firm. You are not ignoring your customers with food and beverage's strategy as long as you do market research to reality test your products.

Thus, it was decided. They settled on a brief statement that they decided to add to the mission statement:

The Palmer Madison Avenue Hotel commits all its energies to providing the very best services and the greatest comfort and joy to the most discerning visitors to New York.

The discussion was over by their first afternoon break. Lorna was speechless with awe for the process. How powerful! How magnificent it was to make a decision with a team.

Brian was taking notes in the corner of the nearly empty room. He looked up over his reading glasses.

"How did you do?" he asked.

"It seemed to be OK," she said cautiously. "I think maybe I could have had more control. It was...Brian, it was fun."

"I like the way you kept your own opinion out of it," he said, "and your enthusiasm for their participation was wonderful, without tipping your hand or taking sides. Only once you said to Sam, 'I think that's great!'"

Lorna nodded. "I remember that. Things slowed down for a few minutes after that. I'm sure everyone was wondering if what they had said was not so great."

"Right," Brian said. "I also liked the way you verified."

"Eh?"

"You repeated what others said occasionally to make sure everyone was clear regarding a point. It also let the person who made the point think about what they had said.

"Now, let's talk about the next section. It may be a little more complicated because the question is not going to be so clear. If it's all right with you, I will explain a concept then pass the baton to you. In the last hour you were deciding between choices. This time you will generate lists."

Brian wrote on the board:

KEY FACTORS FOR SUCCESS

"I will define what this means, and then you ask them what they think they are."

He wrote on the top of the next page:

OUR STRONGEST COMPETITORS

On a third page he wrote:

OUR COMPETITORS' GREATEST WEAKNESSES

"After you have done this, you will see that some of our greatest strengths counter some of our competitors' greatest weaknesses.

"After this exercise you should be able to make some strategic decisions."

He wrote **"STRATEGIES"** on a fourth page.

After the break, Brian spoke briefly to the group.

"One of the best strategic thinkers, I know," Brian said, "is Dr. Kenuche Ohmae."

"One of his most impressive concepts is the idea that organizations should understand and build on their Key Factors for Success.

"Dr. Ohmae, in his book *The Mind of the Strategist*, says:

> *The point in this method is to identify the key factors for success (KFS) in the industry or business concerned and then to inject a concentration of resources into a particular area where the company sees an opportunity to gain its most significant strategic advantage over its competitors. Even when the company has in effect no more management resources than its competitors, in the same business or trade, it can often achieve resounding competitive success if its effective in bringing those resources to bear on the one crucial point. I call this method, business strategy based on KFS.*

"What does this mean?" asked Brian.

"I am really taken with this idea, if I understand it correctly," said Bill. "It means identifying what we do well and emphasizing this area."

The discussion continued for a few minutes. Finally, an exasperated Sam said, "Yes, but what are the key factors for our success? We are all concerned with how poorly the hotel is doing. Maybe we don't have any."

Brian stood up. "Great question. This afternoon is our last session together for a few weeks. I suggest we answer that question and try to begin formulating a strategy for developing the best hotel in New York."

When Brian had finished his little lecture, he sat down and Lorna stood up by the flip chart. She flipped the pages over until she got to **"KEY FACTORS FOR SUCCESS."** "What are the key factors for our success?" she asked.

"Size, we already agreed on that one," said Sarah.

Perfect Service

Lorna wrote the word down and said, "Listen, I need somebody to do this for me."

"Can't you walk and chew gum at the same time?" asked Chet.

Lorna said, "You just volunteered," and tossed the marker at him.

Lorna asked, "Why is size so important?"

"Because it enables us to remember guests' names and allows us to give them special services that we couldn't give in a larger house," said Joan. "Also, guests are less intimidated by smaller hotels."

"Location," said Walter. "We are in both a residential neighborhood and in the midtown financial area."

"Restaurant," said Andy. "Why?" asked Lorna.

"The size allows it to accommodate more customers than the guests who would normally use it," he said.

"Another advantage of the restaurant," he added, "is that there is an outside entrance separate from the guest entrance."

"Rooms," said Ruth.

"Why?"

"High ceilings, fairly good size bathrooms, nice old fixtures."

"I am not sure that my department would agree with you," Chet said over his shoulder.

"When they work," added Ruth. "Also windows that open."

"A hard core of really great guests," said Fred, "and also a hard core of really great employees."

"One at a time," Lorna said as the engineer wrote furiously.

Sam looked at Sarah. "How many guests would you say are steady, of high quality and are people we would very much like to bring with us if we upgrade the hotel?"

Sarah said, "I have been trying to figure that out. There are at least three hundred people who use the hotel more than four times a year and with an average stay of approximately three nights. They are not rate resistant. In the last increase it appears that we lost practically none of them."

"Do you have any idea what their pattern is for eating in the dining rooms?" asked Walter.

"Not yet," said Sarah.

"We could figure that out," said Sam. "It's an interesting question."

"I bet we'd find out that a lot of them not only eat in the dining room regularly but invite people in," Lorna said.

"Where are they from?" asked Chet.

"I am embarrassed. I don't know that either, but quite a few are from Europe, a few are from Japan and other parts of Asia, and a lot seem to be from the West Coast," said Sarah.

"What do they like about the hotel?" asked Lorna.

Sarah was scribbling frantically on a piece of paper.

"I don't know that either," she said, "but we'll find out."

"If we are talking about the same people," said Joan, "they are very easy to work with. They let us know when they are coming. Sometimes we keep bags of clothes for them. And they always seem to want the same room."

Andy added, "Sometimes they have special parties in their room or in their suites. They are easy to work with because they know what they want. They often cater parties with their friends using the meeting rooms. I think they are our target market."

"Do we have any other key factors for success?" asked Lorna.

"Palmer reservation service," said John.

"Any others?"

"History. The hotel has a delightful history."

"Meeting rooms. They're small, just suited for the types of groups and functions we cater to. Also, the lobby is pretty and elegant. It's not enormous and overwhelming."

Lorna then led a lively discussion on the competition, which included a number of well-known New York hotels.

Looking at the two lists which Chet had taped to the wall, Lorna asked them to identify areas where the hotel was strong against weaknesses of its competition; their small size, their lack of debt service, the Palmer reservation system, their staff. The group agreed the Palmer Hotel was stronger in all these respects.

"OK," Lorna said. The whole exercise had taken less than half an hour.

"We have decided we are product-driven, and we have reviewed some of our strategic assets. Now, let's make some strategic decisions."

"Let's get a new scribe," said Chet.

"No, you're doing fine," said Fred.

"Another volunteer," said Bill. The personnel director was nominated by acclamation.

First, the group refined the "never sell out" concept; and Fred wrote on the flip chart page marked **"STRATEGIC DECISIONS"**:

> **1. Never sell more than ninety-percent of available rooms.**

Next, the group moved on to a discussion of "authority."

Walter suggested, "Let food and beverage employees 'comp' the meal if the customer doesn't like it."

"That'll never work," said Sam. "The word will get around and half of New York will be here looking for a complimentary meal."

"Not if we train the waiters," said Walter.

After a heated discussion, they adopted a strategy that all service people could 'comp' up to the value of the service they provided. If the guest was unhappy, then no questions would be asked by management, except for analytical purposes. Considerable thought and four pieces of flip chart paper went into the writing of the strategy.

> **2. From January fifteenth, if a staff member feels that a service he or she provides has a reduced value to a guest then he or she can reduce the cost up to the value of that service.**

Next the group discussed and refined their target market.

"Our biggest problem is that most of our room nights are not generated by those five hundred people Sarah mentioned earlier," said Walter. "We have become a group hotel. We have airlines, overflow groups from the convention hotels, including the Palmer New York, incentive groups, tour groups, etc.
The groups tend to overwhelm the individual traveler. They're easier to sell. However, the more groups you have, the fewer individual travelers you get. And your services tend to be geared to groups.

"For example," he continued, "I would love to tap into the New York 'power' breakfast, lunch, and dinner crowd. But they hardly ever show up at the hotel because our restaurants are geared to high volume."

"So, let's review who we want as our guest," Lorna said. After discussion, Fred wrote down:

3. **Focus marketing efforts and hotel products on the following guest (target market profile):**
   - **Individual**
   - **Able to pay our rates**
   - **Demands quality**
   - **Expects anonymity**
   - **Visits several times a year**
   - **Has long-term need to be in New York**

"How are we going to find all of these people?" asked Chet.

"That is going to be a problem," said Sarah. "It seems to me, we have already agreed to do a better analysis of our existing individual guest. Once we know more, we can build a product that will attract them over and over again. When we get a critical mass of such people, they will attract others."

The next strategy related to focused sales efforts. It was decided that their primary sales effort would be geared toward New York, with the assumption being that New Yorkers influence the decisions of which hotel their out-of-town visitors stay in.

4. **Focus sales efforts on New York.**
   - **Build local restaurant following**
   - **Build local beverage following**
   - **Build catering**
   - **Build rooms**

They discussed the secondary market strategy, which was to advertise extensively in comparable Palmer Hotels. Palmer has a potpourri of hotels all over the world, some extraordinarily beautiful and comparable to the Madison Avenue in size, some enormous convention hotels and some roadside motels.

5. Advertise in comparable Palmer Hotels.

The decisions came quickly after that.

6. Join the small luxury hotels association (if they will have us).

7. Major refurbishing of all rooms — floor by floor — filling these rooms at premium rates as completed. Involve staff in process.

8. Develop and publicize secretarial services.

9. Develop an extensive health center and spa.

Their discussion also focused on their "second market," the staff.

10. Never lay off employees; reduce staff only by attrition or termination for cause.

11. Cease massive inspection within six months.

12. No employee works without supervision until they have been through two weeks minimum training.

There was considerable conversation and dissention on this point. The group decided that it would take three months for this to go into effect as no basic training programs had been developed for line staff.

13. Within six months, all staff to be certified to have attained skills in all requisite jobs. All managers are certified in the same skills as the jobs they supervise.

14. The Palmer Madison Avenue Hotel wil constantly involve all staff in making improvements.
Every department will meet once a week to discuss improvement.

By this time the sun had dropped over the tops of the hills. It was agreed to close the meeting, as they all had a long drive back to New York.

"Before we leave," Lorna said, "I would like to say a couple of words. For me, and I hope for the rest of you, this weekend will be a major turning point. I realized two things this weekend more than anything else. First, how incredibly fortunate I am to work with all of you, and with you, Brian, and with you, John. Second, how much affection we all have for the old building in which we work and how much dedication we have to making it live up to its potential. This is a very exciting experience for me and I know we will work even harder in the months to come."

She sat down to tumultuous applause. John stood.

"I have learned more about the hotel in the last two days," he said "than I have in the last ten years. I know what really makes it work — the staff and the management team. I also have gotten a clear picture of the systems and strategies of the old days, which inhibited us from really living up to our potential, both as individuals and as a team. I hope I can stand by you in the future, listen to you, get your complaints and suggestions, encourage you to continue the path you've chosen here. Finally, I am deeply grateful that you invited me to this meeting. It was a strategy of risk on Lorna's part and I promise I will never tell anyone at Palmer that I came here." He then walked quietly around the room and shook each person's hand, addressing them by name, and thanking them for their participation. When, at last, he reached Lorna, he said, "Lorna, I look forward to working with you as a partner in the next few months. It is going to be very exciting."

Lorna thanked him. They agreed to meet every other Tuesday for lunch.

They religiously honored this engagement throughout the turbulent months that followed.

chapter
XVIII

Homecoming

Lorna returned to the hotel in a state of euphoria.

Early Monday morning she had coffee in the employees' cafeteria with three early arriving waitresses from the coffee shop. They were friendly but wary and more nervous about appearing to be too cozy with management than about Lorna herself. They were tough, crusty New Yorkers who had families in Queens and had been through a great deal to keep them together.

Lorna asked how things had gone over the weekend.

"The hotel ran better without you guys than it does normally," one said, only half jokingly.

"Listen," asked Lorna, ignoring the remark. "What are things that keep us from having perfect service in the restaurant in the morning?"

"Perfect service, forget it, what about Joe's Diner service?" said one. "Too many customers all at once. Guests always arrive in a big bunch at 7:15 and no one seems ready for them. You get a long line out the door of the place and at the same time a lot of empty tables. The guests always complain about that."

"Why aren't you ready?" Damn, thought Lorna, I'm trying to lay blame.

"It's not our fault, Miss Johnson. It's the way we're scheduled. That's management's problem."

"Forget fault," Lorna said, realizing that a few weeks ago, she would have looked for fault herself. "What are some of the causes of the problem?"

"What I just said. We're all scheduled to arrive at the same time."

"The evening people should get the dining room ready for breakfast."

"The flatware isn't clean. You have to reject a lot of it, and you have to wipe a lot of it off. You have to spend a lot of time checking it. That's what we're going to do now."

"Not enough staff."

"There go your tips," said another.

"I bet we lose more business and tips from the way things are now."

"Everyone waits for the hostess. She can only go back and forth so fast."

"The kitchen gets backlogged and they forget orders."

"Yeah, and a certain person, whose name begins with M for Mildred, steals other people's orders."

"Why can't we seat the guests ourselves?"

"Because you'd grab all the fat cats for your own section."

Lorna began writing down the comments, thinking about Brian's three steps.

"How would you ideally like to see the dining room?"

"No line."

"Everything coming out of the kitchen on time, as ordered."

"Relaxed, friendly."

"Flexible, like we get three orders a week for capuccino. Nobody knows how to work the machine so we say the machine is broken. Hell, I say give them capuccino."

"Come on, Millie, I don't want to know how to run the capuccino machine. It takes too long."

"But we should be able to meet the needs of the guests."

The waitresses stood up. "We've got to go or management will be on our back," one said. The others laughed.

Lorna was ecstatic. None of the ideas were expensive and if they could reduce the line, that would have a dramatic impact on the way they served breakfast.

She had long felt that breakfast in the coffee shop was where the biggest impact on the guests was made.

For many, it was their last meal before check out. For others, it was a time to informally conduct business.

She was also struck by the fact that most of the suggestions were geared toward pleasing the customers, not toward making life easier for the union help.

The waitresses spent most of their time with the guests.

chapter
XIX

Meetings

For the first three weeks very little changed in the hotel from the standpoint of the guests and the staff. The latter, however, felt a stirring of a fresh breeze blowing through the old building. Every department head began to hold meetings every week. Initially these meetings were stumbling and chaotic in most departments.

The department heads who had been in Vermont (The Green Mountain Gang) sensed that there was a rift of culture between themselves and the line staff.

"There is no trust," said one. "They don't even trust us. I asked the staff who had taken the initiative the other day to buy flowers for Mrs. Ross, a long-term guest, and they wouldn't tell me. I just wanted to thank them and they still wouldn't tell me."

Some staff even resented being taken away from "my guests" for the meeting.

By agreement, the first meetings were primarily informational. In the first week, the department heads gave out carefully prepared highlights of financial results for the previous month and had some discussion. In the second week, they reviewed the mission statement with the employees and asked the employees to discuss it among themselves and be prepared to review it in the third meeting. On Thursday afternoon each week, the entire Green Mountain Gang met and reviewed the meetings, department by department, and offered each other suggestions.

In general, there was little participation in the department meetings, the group concluded. The meetings seemed totally different from the sessions in Vermont. Few employees participated at all and those who did would often ramble, repeat themselves or clown around. Only the youngest and newest employees seemed to speak constructively. Ironically, some of them seemed to pull back after the first meeting. Perhaps other members of the group warmed them into silence.

At the Green Mountain Gang's suggestion, Brian came in one Saturday and ran a workshop on facilitation. He showed a number of taped vignettes of actual meetings and demonstrated facilitation skills with them. Each person had a chance to facilitate a session. These sessions were videotaped and played back, much to the agony and amusement of the participants.

chapter
XX

Training

In December, a firm was brought in to train department heads in a three-day program called "Training For Results." *

The trainers were all experienced in hotel operations. They were demanding and tough, and the course was designed to compress as much experience as possible into the three days.

Each trainee had to give a series of presentations to the group. These were videotaped and heavily critiqued.

The amount of preparation required for the course was exhausting and the group soon gave up trying to run their departments by remote control during the three days.

At the end of the course, the entire group, led by Lorna, gave the trainers a standing ovation.

For the next two months, the trainers worked two days a week in the hotel helping the department heads develop detailed written standards and procedures for each job. This was an exhaustive effort. Some

*Copyright Victoria International Corporation, Boston, Mass.

department heads involved line employees, and a few particularly creative department heads videotaped their standards with the help of the training director. Lorna met briefly each day with Bill Holtzman, the training manager, and, when they were in the hotel, the trainers.

Lorna had insisted on reviewing the standards and procedures for each job. The training consultants provided her with exhaustive hotel industry checklists. In some cases the standards were already prepared by another training firm. * Lorna let some of the divisional work slip while she was reviewing the standards and procedures.

Her boss in the regional office gave her several lectures about becoming a paper pusher.

This was a difficult time for Lorna. She was inundated with piles of paper. Department heads always seemed to have some excuse for not completing the standards on time. The region was constantly on her back for trivial things. Her operating costs seemed to be creeping up, while her guest comments and average room rate seemed to decline.

Even her best friend and political ally in the regional office, Janice Skilcroft, seemed unavailable to counsel her and warn her in advance when the mud was about to fly.

Brian, John, Maria Luisa, and Lorna's mother got her through this time. The two Wolcott daughters often dropped by her office to share a chocolate chip cookie with her. They had both decided to become hotel general managers. They all helped her present a calm, supportive, cheerful face to the Green Mountain Gang.

Bill Holtzman blossomed during the first six months. He had been very frustrated earlier.

Of twenty training managers in the region, only two had worked more than one year in that position. It was considered a minefield. The position itself was forced on general managers by Palmer and they were asked to put the training manager on their executive committee. In many cases, department heads stopped what little training they were doing when the training manager was appointed, rationalizing that the training department was now responsible. Initially, training managers found it difficult to convince even personnel directors that training could really make a difference.

Many of the line managers that Palmer had imported from other countries had little faith in training, particularly for minority workers. Most of them had been trained through a painful ordeal of apprenticeships where they spent years at the bottom of the ladder, and many of them believed that there was only one way to the top — suffering. They were appalled at the American unwillingness to suffer.

*The Freeman Group, Dallas, Tex.

Perfect Service

Few Palmer managers had learned their jobs in a manner that a professional trainer would consider useful or efficient. They learned by working long hours, by observing others, and above all, by being corrected — often in public, by impatient bosses. As they shifted from one boss to another they noted that personal preferences changed dramatically, so they might get chewed out by one boss for doing something exactly the way the last boss wanted it.

Seldom were procedures written down. What was available were fifth-generation photocopies of a manual from another hotel chain. There was nothing for a new employee to read or study about his or her job.

Hands-on training for new employees was often done not by a manager (who was far too busy dealing with the results of improper training), but by a fellow employee using the "trailer" system: "Go trail Maggie for a couple of days and if you have any questions, ask her."

Ironically, in an industry whose value in the customers' eyes is created by friendly, attentive, confident, and competent service employees, few workers had friendly, attentive, confident, and competent bosses to emulate. The training process for most of the front line workers was characterized by rejection, rather than fostering feelings of acceptance.

Bill felt that the ball game had changed drastically. No longer the bat boy, he had been promoted to coach.

chapter XXI
Leadership

Lorna finally had approved all the standards and procedures. It had been a massive job and the intensive training of new staff had begun long before the jobs were fully defined. At first, the results were mixed. The personnel director gave a short report at one of the Green Mountain Gang meetings showing that turnover had actually increased as the training program was implemented and that more, rather than fewer, people left during their first few weeks of training.

Lorna called Brian, who was in San Diego working with a large retail chain. "Keep up the same effort, Lorna," he advised. "First, you don't know if there is a problem; there is little data to tell, and it is a big mistake to react too quickly when the training program is so new. Second, you should start seeing a reduction in turnover among employees who stay longer." The training consultants agreed and Lorna continued to take a very strong and supportive posture regarding the training.

But the bills were adding up. The consultants' fees were high but this was a minor cost compared to the "unproductive time" it cost to bring in employees for training. Sam kept very close track of the costs.

At the same time, Lorna was having a major tug of war with the regional office over her "strategic plan." The strategic planning process was geared to producing numbers first and justifying those numbers later. Lorna had submitted a plan that was "strong on concept and weak on numbers," according to the regional controller. She had projected a modest increase in revenues and an equal increase in expenses to offset training costs and bringing in more staff to augment coverage in such key areas as front desk and telephone. The regional controller wanted her to take the difference to the bank. "You know you can run with low costs of operation," he said. "Why don't you keep a tight ship? You keep the expenses down and you'll look like a hero. Also, what happens if your expenses go up and the dollar gets strong again? Then you will be squeezed because your average room rate will sag and you are stuck with lazy employees. You can always give something to your staff, Lorna, but you can't take it away."

She finally called John into the picture. He wrote her an innocent letter complaining about times that fictitious friends had tried to reach the hotel only to have the phone ring several times. He got a friend from the CTX board to complain to Palmer Hotels about a slow check-out line. These solved the problem when the regional vice president of operations called Lorna saying he had gotten a call from the chairman himself that morning. "For God's sake, get in more staff," he told her. They were under negotiation with CTX to purchase a property in Chicago from an insurance company and they could not afford one single complaint about poor service in their luxury hotels.

Lorna was astonished at the quick results and her new strategic plan was approved without further comment from the regional controller. She wondered if he suspected complicity, but if so, he probably would never figure out how it happened. She was very pleased that none of the Green Mountain Gang had ever mentioned to anyone that John had participated in their weekend retreat. Her direct line to John was completely unknown to Palmer Hotels and the entire Green Mountain Gang planned to keep it that way.

These skirmishes were very tiring to Lorna. She knew that acceptance of her strategic plan was at best a Pyrrhic victory. She had drawn fire on her own position and the chairman himself might begin taking shots at her.

Little did she know how certain that possibility was.

chapter
XXII

The Gathering

By the end of six months, every employee had been certified in all the tasks required to perform his or her job. The certification process itself was a nightmare because no matter how tactfully the process was handled, the older employees felt insulted that they were being tested and fearful that it would somehow affect their jobs.

Lorna began a series of monthly meetings with the entire hotel's staff. John agreed to kick off the first meeting. All the employees knew him by sight but really didn't know him as a person. With Bill's coaching, he had some excellent graphics prepared for the overhead projector. He carefully thought through what he was going to say.

"I am very pleased to be here," he began, "and I am particularly pleased that representatives of the union have joined us today."

There was laughter for a few seconds, then it became apparent that he was serious as he put his hand lightly on the shoulder of the business agent who shared the podium.

"Johnny DelGado has been through a great deal in our industry," he continued.

"He worked as a shoeshine porter when he was fifteen years old in the old Commodore Hotel. He became a bellman after a great struggle because in those days jobs were scarce and there was a great deal of injustice in the hotel industry in New York."

"There still is," said Johnny.

"I agree," said John, to everyone's surprise.

He continued, "Johnny was a good bellman from what I have heard. But he soon realized that he could not be loyal to his customers, his fellow workers, his growing family, and to management at the same time. This became painfully clear whenever there was a slowdown in business and he was laid off. I'm sure we all know what it's like trying to please people whose interests contradict each other." There were murmurs of assent. Lorna noticed that the audience was suddenly paying very close attention to John.

"As you may know, my grandfather built this hotel. Like Johnny, he was a self-made man. He left a farm in Massachusetts at a young age because his family farm had failed and the banks had foreclosed. My grandfather came to New York and took any job he could to be able to send money back to his mother and sisters who lived in poverty in Palmer, Massachusetts. He slept on the floor of a tavern in the Wall Street area where he washed dishes and did odd jobs. Eventually, through good fortune and hard work, he became a trader. Frankly, I'm not sure I want to know what he traded, but he had the reputation of being tough and politically well-connected, and he prospered, losing and making several fortunes. He died two years after finishing the hotel in 1931. He had made wise investments and the family survived the depression, and we somehow held onto the hotel.

"My father, who was born late in my grandfather's life, had no interest in the hotel. He let other people run it. You old-timers know that it went through a series of ups and downs, and you know what it was like to try to do your job without much support from my family.

"As you may know, our family is a large one now and has a lot of different interests. I have been the person who has decided to represent the family and to take an active interest in this hotel.

"In recent times, I have asked myself why are we always at odds with the employees of the hotel? Why have there been so many grievances? Why do our occupancy and our revenues go through such violent changes from one week to the next?

"I've concluded that we are at each other's throats because we are victims of a common problem. The problem is that we are at the mercy of our market, and we are doing nothing to make our hotel a stable environment.

"I began to realize that our purpose as a business is to give the greatest value to our customers, to provide you with the best possible careers, to be a good citizen in the community, and to provide my family with a profit. If we focus first on the profit, however, we won't be able to achieve the other three.

"If we have a really good system in the hotel we can achieve all of this. I see my job as providing you with a physical product that you can be proud of. Your job is to treat each other and your guests with the utmost kindness and responsiveness.

"A recent study I saw showed that when customers don't return, sixty-eight percent of the time it's because of indifference on the part of the employees. I know how hard it is to present a positive cheerful attitude when you don't have the tools you need to give your customers what they want.

"That's where management comes in. Their primary job is to listen carefully to our guests and to establish standards. Next, they are responsible for letting you know what those standards are. That's why there is so much training going on in the hotel. Third, their job is to support you and help you get the tools needed to do the job effectively. Finally, staff and management have a collective responsibility to work together to solve problems, and improve constantly and forever the way we serve our guests.

"For example, I heard that a front desk clerk the other day went out during her lunch break and bought flowers for one of our long-staying guests because it was her birthday. The controller of the hotel wants to reimburse her and no one at the front desk will admit to doing it and even the guest won't tell us who gave her the flowers.

"I am concerned about what this means for us as a family. When there is so much fear and mistrust, we all suffer," John paused. The room was completely silent.

"First, we must evolve a system by which we always remember our long-time guests' birthdays and automatically send them flowers or a gift or even have a party for them in the dining room. Second, there are always things you, as employees, are asked to do or think of doing on your own to improve the guest's experience. We should always let you respond to these opportunities for excellence and provide you with the support you need.

"Now, this effort is already underway." He paused for effect and drew a folded piece of paper from his pocket. "This," he unfolded it, "is a letter of agreement from U.S. Trust in Boston to loan us fifteen million dollars for a renovation of all of our rooms and the back-of-the-house."

Even Johnny joined the applause. One of the maintenance engineers stood up and said, "It's about time!"

John continued, "I would like to show you a slide of the letter."

"Now, you notice my signature on the bottom. You know how banks are. They don't give you money because they like you or because you are a good citizen or because you have a wonderful idea. They give you money because they have no risk in loaning it to you. With my signature on this document, it means that I am committing the building and all of my personal assets as collateral to this loan. That way, they have passed the risk over to me and you.

"We are going to try to do this rehab floor by floor without closing the hotel. This will make it more expensive, but the basic building is in good shape and we think we can do the rehab with a minimum of disruption to the guests.

"There is no doubt, however, that the renovation is going to be hard on you, and I am counting on you to continually improve the quality of our services under very difficult circumstances." He paused. "Can you do that?"

There were a few murmurs.

John turned toward Johnny. "Do you think they can do this?" he asked jokingly.

"They always have, in spite of managers coming and going," replied Johnny, smiling. There was laughter.

John turned back to the audience. "So, can you do it?"

This time one of the room attendants yelled from the back of the room, "Yes, Mr. Wolcott."

"I'm sorry, I still can't hear you," he said. "Can you do it?"

This time the response was deafening. When the tumult settled down, John introduced Lorna.

"We are very fortunate," he said, "to have a leader in this effort who is a great hotelier and who shares your vision of how the hotel should be. Most important, she has an open mind and really believes that the needs of our guests, staff, management, owners and community can be meshed, as we become the very best hotel in New York."

Lorna stood up to perfunctory applause, and began to speak. Johnny DelGado did not join the applause.

"Johnny made a comment about managers coming and going and I am very sensitive to this comment. For this reason, like it or not, you are going to have me here for at least the next five years. I want to see this through."

Johnny interrupted, "The devil you know is better than the one you don't know." Lorna smiled. The audience laughed.

"The most important assets of this hotel are the loyalty of our staff and the loyalty of our customers, and the two are tied together. Many of you have been here through thick and thin, and all during that time, no matter who managed the hotel, you remained loyal to your customers. Sometimes I'm sure you treated your customers well in spite of the treatment that you yourselves felt you were receiving from management. The next few months will test this loyalty because it's very difficult to work in a building that is being renovated.

"As I have mentioned to you, we are blessed with a beautiful building. We are fortunate to have an owner who is willing to take big risks and renovate the building to bring it up to date. The guests, however, do not judge a book by its cover. They judge it by how they are treated by all of us.

"We have begun to realize that in order to perfect our services, we must free you up to enable you to respond to the opportunities for perfect service that your guests give you.

"You are in the middle of a training program to make sure that you are completely comfortable with all of the many skills required in your jobs. For some of you, this may seem like old hat. After a while, however, you will find that you will be learning new tricks. It's particularly important that we help new employees master the skills required in their jobs, and that you support and help them. As we improve the systems and services, you will get more and more training.

"Now," she paused, "how many of you have wanted to take a course and learn something new?" Initially only a few hands went up. Lorna waited patiently while more and more hands went up. "I would like to ask Johnny DelGado to talk with us about our external education program."

Johnny rose to a round of applause.

"You will be pleased to know that in cooperation with the union, the

Palmer Madison Avenue Hotel has allocated five hundred dollars for each person each year to help pay for any course you want to take that will help you in your job or will help you to advance into another job in the hotel. For example, you may want to improve your English or your reading and writing skills, or you may want to take a course in advanced mathematics or computer programming. The union and the training department have catalogues of courses for you to look at, and this morning, course announcements have been posted on the bulletin board. I have talked with Miss Johnson about the program and I am convinced that management is sincere in its efforts to help you get ahead."
He went on to make some union announcements and fielded some questions.

Lorna walked back up to the podium.

"In conclusion, the next few months are going to be very exciting. We will be working together to rebuild our hotel. At times, it is going to be difficult and disruptive. We will need the following from you.

"First, listen carefully to our guests for ways that we can improve our hotel. Some of you are not dealing directly with the hotel's guests. But every one of us has customers. If you are working in the kitchen, who is your customer?"

"The waiter," shouted a steward.

"Right. And if you work in the laundry, who is your customer?"

"The room attendant."

"So, find out what your customers need and share your ideas with your boss in your weekly meeting.

"Second, do everything you can to bring the guest back. Take more latitude in your jobs. If a guest needs something and, if by giving it, you will help the hotel in the long run, then take the initiative and make sure they get it. Of course, make sure that it's legal," she said, looking at three bellpersons sitting in the front row. There was laughter from the group.

"Third, learn as much as you can. The hotel business is changing rapidly. Customers expect more and more from us. We are like lawyers or doctors. We need to continually keep up with our field. In the next few days, you will take a wonderful course called T.I.G.E.R. * I have taken the course, and it helped me a great deal to understand other people's needs. You will enjoy the class and you will find that it helps you as much in the hotel as it does in the rest of your life.

"Only very recently," she concluded, "have I begun to realize how much more valuable we can be to each other. Too often we have created mistrust and fear among each other. I have been afraid that you would make me look bad in the eyes of Palmer or the owner. You have been afraid, sometimes for your jobs.

*Training In Guest Employee Relations. Copyright Victoria International Corporation, Boston, Mass.

Let's do what we can to eliminate fear from our work lives. There is no reason to be fearful, if we focus on our customer and help each other to be successful.

"I look forward to working with you in the next few months. There is no doubt that we can achieve our goal. And what is our goal?"

"Make money," shouted a bell person.

"No," Lorna said, "that's a result of achieving our goal. What is our goal?"

"The best hotel in New York."

"Right," Lorna said, "The Best." She shouted the last two words.

Sam Thompson, who was becoming the Green Mountain Gang's ham, stood up in the front row and started chanting "The best!! The best!! The best!!..."

Lorna burst out laughing. He seemed ridiculous standing alone in the room — particularly a controller. Suddenly, one of the bellpersons stood up and took up the chant and turned toward the staff urging them to get up and the chant spread through the room as people began standing. Johnny and John sat bewildered on the head table.

Suddenly John reached over and grabbed Johnny's arm and they both stood up together and joined the chant. Lorna was dumbfounded. An enormous room attendant made her way chanting and clapping to the front of the room and stood in front of Lorna as if instructing her how to chant and clap. Slowly, tentatively, Lorna joined in. The chant died being replaced by tumultuous applause. Lorna grabbed the room attendant's hand and held it aloft. The room attendant reached over and grabbed Johnny's hand. The four stood in front of the group for a long time chanting and laughing.

"The best!! The best!! The best!!"

chapter
XXIII

the Renovation

The meeting had an immediate impact on lessening the tension between management and staff. The department meetings took on a new life. The Green Mountain Gang had decided to focus these meetings on the renovation project. Each department was required to come up with a plan. Staff members began to contribute extensively to the plan and Lorna noticed that the weekly departmental meetings were being supplemented by informal groups of staff gathering on their own, looking at plans.

When it came time for the Green Mountain Gang to review the departmental plans three weeks later, some department heads brought staff members in to make the presentations. A room attendant found herself in front of the group working with a flip chart for the first — and she hoped — last time in her life.

Lorna, who was in a state of continuous amazement, found that the plans were extremely well thought through and contained a level of detail she had never seen in previous construction projects.

From the initial presentations, which proved to her the value of collaboration, she began integrating the interior designers, architects, engineers, her staff, and marketing people into the discussions. She told her mother that she had become the "grande facilitator." But that role was short-lived. At her insistence, the project manager appointed by Palmer began attending many of the departmental meetings. A cynical former hotel engineer, he was skeptical about the process. He told his wife there were so many hands in the pie that he would be lucky to be done in ten years. When he saw how well the departments were planning, however, he began to get caught up in the collaborative spirit. When he wasn't in meetings, he opened his office to the public. At Lorna's encouragement, he gradually took over the role of the grande facilitator himself in the discussions between the various professionals involved.

The role of the marketing department in the planning process was critical. As promised, Sarah had put together a detailed profile of the ideal guest and, aided by the Palmer marketing department, had determined the needs and preferences of this guest.

Sarah had also conducted a series of focus groups with individuals who met this profile and with New Yorkers who were likely to recommend visitors to stay in the hotel. These groups reviewed the plans of the interior decorators and architects. Sarah took detailed notes and with Brian's help was able to assemble a statistical profile of the key quality indicators of this group.

The ranking showed the following to be the key quality indicators:

1. Clean rooms and facilities.

2. Friendly, attentive service geared to my particular needs.

3. Excellent food but not too "far out." (Sarah conducted her focus groups over lunch or dinner and the groups tested menu items. The chef, a very creative Californian, was disappointed in their response to his "Mussel Pâte" and his "Blackened Venison in Stilton Cheese Sauce.")

4. Consistency in product.

5. Health and recreational facilities.

6. Privacy.

7. Individual business services — a private secretary.

When shown a model room, the guests liked the warmth and elegance, but they also were insistent on desks that they could write on, with a two-line telephone. They wanted a fax machine in each room. They wanted two regular chairs to sit at for room service meals. They were unimpressed with the telephone and television in the bathroom but loved the deep tub and separate shower stall. They wanted brighter lighting. They were impressed with the remote controlled hi-fi set with four speakers, but they also wanted a video cassette player with a library of movies. Sarah noted that they did not ask for some products when interviewed prior to going to the room, but liked them once they saw them. Brian told her that was natural. "Sometimes you lead the consumer and other times you only respond to them," he said. She urged everyone in the hotel to think of new services that would separate the hotel from its competition.

Within one month, John found himself going back to the bank for an additional two million dollars. He brought with him the data generated by Palmer and the hotel's sales and marketing staff. This information was very compelling to John and his confidence was growing by the minute. Because the hotel was relatively free of debt, he realized that he could build a luxury product for a fraction of the cost that others were putting into New York hotels. He could charge lower rates and still make money.

Lorna realized that involving so many members of the community, the guests and the staff in the project, was helping to cement tremendous loyalty in both the labor market and the guest market.

The work involved was tremendous. As Sarah learned more and more about the needs of customers and as employees became more involved, the department heads found that many of the standards and procedures they had worked on so hard needed to be changed to accommodate new services.

"When will it end?" Lorna asked Brian.

"What do you think?" he asked back.

chapter
XXIV

T.I.G.E.R.

T.I.G.E.R., which stands for Training In Guest Employee Relations, seemed a curious acronym to the Green Mountain Gang. The employees, however, completely accepted the idea and the course from the outset, partly because it was presented by outside training professionals who had worked in hundreds of other hotels. Mainly, however, the course was effective because of the way the material was presented.

The instructors insisted on working with small groups. From the first fifteen minutes of the course, the students were drawn into intense discussion on every subject presented. Everything the students said was challenged. Within a short time, they returned the fire and challenged everything the instructor said. The students were constantly asked to refer to their own experience. This helped them internalize the concepts. Lorna, John, and all the Green Mountain Gang sat through the course with different groups of staff. This made the staff nervous at first, but when staff members saw their managers struggling with the same concepts, the barrier disappeared.

To Lorna, the course boiled down to four concepts: acceptance, harmony, understanding, and success.

Throughout the course, the instructors used videotaping to let the employees see themselves as their customers saw them. The course focused on a series of "microskills." Each of the four concepts of the course required the practice of skills.

John Wolcott particularly found the concepts very moving. At the dinner table he shared one of the concepts with Maria Luisa and their two daughters.

"It is time I explained to you children about the concept of acceptance," he said with mock seriousness. "Acceptance means that I approve of you even when you don't do your homework, or your mother approves of me even when I forget to schedule an appointment for her."

"Never," said his wife teasingly, "and I never forget."

John smiled and continued, "I approve of you as a human being and I respect your right to exist. People have a basic need to be approved by each other. People always seek approval from others and try to avoid rejection. Maybe this is a basic need because people have to cooperate to survive. We are not like some other animals who are alone most of the time and hunt for food by themselves. We specialize; you fish and I farm."

"Where do lawyers fit in?" asked Maria Luisa.

"They hunt," said John.

"No wonder there are so many endangered species."

Just as the instructor had done, John asked his children for examples of rejection. Soon they were overwhelming him with examples from the past.

"Well, for example, yesterday you forgot to tell me that Jonah called. That made me feel rejected."

"You only let us watch two hours of television a week when normal parents let their normal children watch TV all the time."

John covered his face in shame. "I'm so embarrassed," he said. "How do these terrible things make you feel?" he asked, imitating the T.I.G.E.R. instructor.

"Hurt."

"Angry."

"Depressed."

"Lacking in confidence."

John continued, "We are taught from experience that some people's rejection hurts more than others. It might be that if one of your friends who is pretty unreliable anyway forgot to tell you about a phone call you might not be as upset as you are with me. Why?"

"We expect more from you. You are more important to us."

"And you to me. You could do something that would really bother me. If your cousins did the same thing it wouldn't bother me at all."

"Why would it bother you?" asked Francesca.

"Because I might not feel that you respect me, I feel rejected. So, people value some people's opinions more than others."

"Like my teacher, Miss Horsebreath, she can make you feel terrible. I wish I didn't care," said Meredith.

"So, in some funny way," said John, "you look up to her, you want her to approve of you. Now, turn it around. Does she ever get upset with her students?"

"All the time."

"Why?"

"I don't know."

"Maybe she wants the approval of the students. Maybe she sees rejection when it doesn't exist."

"But Daddy, that's weird. Why would a teacher worry about what the students think?" Francesca asked.

John continued, "She worries because you are important to her. In a funny way she looks up to you just the way you look up to her. And don't say you don't look up to her. If she has ever hurt your feelings, that's a sure sign that her approval is important to you."

His daughters were silent, trying to figure a way to use this concept to their advantage in the academic jungle.

"Daddy, now that you have discovered how much you can hurt us, could you let us watch Miami Vice reruns tonight as a way of showing your approval?" asked Meredith.

After the children had left the table, Maria Luisa asked, "What does this concept have to do with the hotel?"

"Many things. The employees should try to give each other as much recognition and respect as possible to show support. They should realize that those they serve look up to them for approval — that they are important in the eyes of others. It doesn't matter if the guest is older or richer or more traveled or better educated. The guest still seeks the approval of the staff, just as the staff seeks the approval of the guest. So, in a funny way, the guest looks up to the employee. Remember when I mentioned that when Americans change their loyalties to another company, sixty-eight percent of the time it is because of indifference on the part of the staff. Indifference is rejection. So, the idea is that no matter what your job, you have customers and your customers need both the services you provide and your acceptance of them as individuals — they have two distinct needs, both related to the other.

"And, if you don't provide the services well, they may see rejection in that, regardless of how nice you are. The instructor did a wonderful demonstration of someone who is friendly and charming but inept. The guest will still feel rejected. So, the message is do your job well and show kindness to those you do it for."

"Who do you do your job for?" she asked out of curiosity.

"My family, I guess."

She smiled. "We can sense that. All of us can. It is wonderful to see how much you have become part of the hotel recently, John. I can feel the difference in the hotel when I go there. When they smile, they genuinely smile. They smile from within."

"It's not me, it's Lorna. And she would tell you it's the staff."

chapter XXV

Harmony

The T.I.G.E.R. concept of harmony was primarily related to emotions. "The job of serving others is always a pressure cooker," explained the trainer. "You are always trying to balance your needs with the needs of your customers, your boss, your family, your fellow workers. This is very stressful and can cause anger, depression, and resentment — often self-directed. This self-directing may add guilt to the emotional pile. Another emotion could be fear.

"Emotions are not something we decide to have. They come to us through our perceptions. We can have the perception that riding in a New York City cab is dangerous, and that can give us emotions of fear. We have a perception that another person is acting disrespectfully toward us, and that can make us feel hurt or rejected, even if rejection was not the intent of the other person.

"Emotions are not our fault. They are triggered by perceptions and perceptions are colored by our experience. We have heard that New York City cab drivers are dangerous, we have read that there are a lot of accidents involving cabs and our experience tells us that going forty miles an hour down Fifth Avenue is dangerous. Our experience dictates fear. A person from Boston, on the other hand, may feel no fear at all in a New York cab because New York drivers are much less reckless than their Boston counterparts.

"Thus, we cannot really control our emotions in the sense of purging them instantly from our system as soon as we have them. You cannot instantly stop anger when you feel it, and people who bury their emotions often find them reappearing at the most embarrassing moments.

"The trick is to deal with extreme, painful emotions as soon as possible, before they have a chance to show their reflection in your behavior. The best system is to talk them out with someone — usually someone you trust and who will not be disrupted in their work."

The trainer pointed out that some cultures find this easier than others. Some cultures view emotion as definitely the fault of the feeler.

chapter XXVI

Graduation

T.I.G.E.R. helped the employees understand their importance to the guests and it helped Lorna implement the hotel's guiding principle of trust, one in which the staff were encouraged to take the initiative and solve problems on their own.

When all the staff had taken the T.I.G.E.R. course, Lorna used the graduation as an opportunity to have another general staff meeting, and she asked John, Johnny DelGado and the training department to present the certificates.

"At last Sunday's brunch," she began, "Jordan Smith from the stewarding department was faced with a request from a guest for cherries jubilee for five of her friends. Jordan left the kitchen and tracked down the duty manager and together they found all the equipment needed to flambé the cherries jubilee. None of the waiters knew how to flambé but one of them had a friend who did. They called the friend at home and he gave them instructions over the phone while they practiced in the kitchen. By this time, the six guests were cheerfully eating their main course.

"The cherries jubilee was a tremendous success. Let's give a hand to this resourceful team." She read off the names of two servers, the manager-on-duty and the dining room manager.

Lorna held up a piece of paper. "Here is Jordan's job description. Does it say on it get equipment and supplies for cherries jubilee on Sunday?"

"No, of course it doesn't. But it does say, perform whatever duties are required to maintain customer satisfaction, and who are Jordan's customers?"

"The chief steward and the chef," came the answer.

"Is that right, Jordan?"

"No," said a shy but obviously pleased Jordan. "It's the servers in the dining room."

"And who are their customers?" asked Lorna.

"The guest."

"Not the dining room manager?"

"The guest."

"So, the server who is serving the guest is also being served by others; for example, the stewarding department. Who else serves the server?" asked Lorna.

"The kitchen."

"Now, Jordan is both a server and a customer. In this example, who served Jordan?"

There was confusion and discussion among the group. Finally one of the room attendants stood up.

"Miss Johnson" she said, "the manager-on-duty did."

"Right, the manager-on-duty!"

"So, this is what we call the chain of service. Some of us are serving the guests. In order for us to serve the guest, we need support from others. The room attendant needs the laundry and the storeroom and the maintenance department, who all help him or her provide the guest with a clean room.

"There often come times for us to do something different, out of the ordinary for the guest, like cherries jubilee, which we don't ordinarily serve for Sunday brunch.

"Last week, for example, a guest who was planning to be here for a week wanted his desk moved over to the window and an extension on the phone so he could make phone calls looking out his window. In our new rooms we will have phones on the desks, but the guest didn't want to wait six months. The room attendant, Marsha Smith, called the maintenance department, after asking the guest's permission to use the phone in his room. The maintenance department sent Jerry Seligman up to the room to help the room attendant move the desk and sent Roland Fontanez out to the electronics store to get an extension cord for the phone. Within twenty minutes the desk was set up exactly as the guest wanted it. This guest is planning to return next month, and the desk and telephone will be ready for him. Our new system should also help us give him the same room.

"In the old days what would have happened, Marsha?" asked Lorna.

"I would have told him to wait until the renovation was complete," said Marsha, "or I would have told him to call my manager."

"The main job of the chain of service is to satisfy our customers and make them come back often, particularly guests like these two," Lorna paused. "You have heard the word authority before, haven't you?"

Lorna was becoming a master at the interactive style of training that she had seen Brian use and that was stressed by the training consultants. One of the staff had suggested that she visit the Abyssinian Baptist Church uptown one Sunday if she really wanted to see how this interactive style worked.

"So, who has authority here in this room?"

"You and Mr. Wolcott," came the answer.

"Yes, we do, and the management team does, including the supervisors. You are forgetting, however, that you also have authority. You have the authority to ensure that your customers' needs are being met, as long as nobody breaks the law or creates a dangerous situation or harms the long-term viability of the business we work for.

"In both the examples I gave you, " Lorna said, "the staff members took the authority necessary to ensure customer satisfaction. They did not have to ask anyone else. The chief engineer was attending a seminar outside the hotel so his staff acted on their own.

"As Mr. Wolcott said in our last meeting, management's job is to give you the tools to be able to exercise your authority in satisfying your customers and to back you up when you respond to some of the special opportunities for excellence that are given to us by our customers.

"Now you have seen a great deal of training taking place, including T.I.G.E.R. This training is to help you feel comfortable in taking more authority in your jobs. Training gives you some of the tools needed to be successful. For example, maybe all the wait staff in the dining room should learn how to flambé cherries jubilee now that the word is getting around the neighborhood.

"So, we are here today to celebrate the training process. Remember, it is a process that is never-ending. There is always more to learn."

John spoke a few words on the renovation. He told them that the planning was almost complete and the bankers kept calling to find out why they had not begun construction. He thanked them for their efforts in helping the planning. He told them that there was going to be another all-employee assembly in a month to review all the plans and asked that each of them visit the model room and comment on it.

Then one of the T.I.G.E.R. graduates spoke. Gabriela LaFontaine was a long-time breakfast cook and she had always been an outspoken advocate of employees' rights. The chef had realized after the Vermont weekend that she was a natural leader and had made her the team leader for the "breakfast brigade," putting her in charge of scheduling staff for the brigade. He had also gotten agreement from the union to give her a small increase in wages. She had blossomed.

"We are here," she began slowly, "to celebrate our graduation from this course, but we are also here to celebrate the fact that once in a while these days management is beginning to use common sense. Miss Johnson, you are not giving us more authority; we had that authority all along and you never let us use it. We have always had our customers and we always wanted to do right by them, but there were times when management got in between us and our customers."

Lorna, sitting in the front of the room, did a pantomime of being shot by an arrow, and lolled her head to one side, closing her eyes. Everyone laughed.

"Time will tell whether this is a little bit of glasnost or a lot of malarkey," Gabriela continued, when the laughter had died down. "But I can say that it's making a big difference. When I was told I had to go to a guest relations program, I had two reactions, both negative. First, I thought, I have not been in school for thirty years and I didn't do so great back then. I have been working all these years without schooling and I got by fine. Second, if I do go to school, I sure as hell don't need to spend two days learning how to smile. Give me something to smile about and you'll see a smile.

"During the course, I began to realize how complicated human relations are and yet how there is a lot we already know that we don't apply. Our teacher was wonderful. She has been in the real world and she learned the T.I.G.E.R. lesson the hard way. She lives the course. You tell her something and she repeats it back to you just like in the course. She shows that she really does understand your emotions and frustrations.

"The thing I liked the most about the course is that it says it's up to us. We don't have to sit around and wait for management to take the initiative or wait for one of the servers, and we are told in the course not to name names, to start being nice before we can be nice to them. I tried accepting him for what he is regardless of his unfriendliness and low and behold Felix...." She clapped her hand to her mouth in mock horror. Everyone looked at Felix, who was doubled over with laughter.

"Even 'no name' started treating me like a human being. So, I want to thank our teacher for this course, and finally I want to thank the managers of this hotel for allowing us to attend the course."

Lorna presented each participant with a T.I.G.E.R. certificate. The whole ceremony was brief but very moving. Several people thanked her and told her not to take it personally.

chapter
XXVII

Sweet & Sour

It was now six months after the Vermont meeting. There had been continuous pressure from the regional office regarding her budget. Lorna's expenses, particularly payroll, had skyrocketed. The regional office had only a vague idea of what Lorna was doing in the hotel. They understood, they said, the importance of training, "but you have guests in the house." One CTX board member had been told by a server that the reason breakfast was so slow was that all the employees were in a session on guest relations. The hammer fell hard on the Palmer Hotels chairman's head and he made sure that it fell even harder on the regional vice president's head, who landed on Lorna with a thorough tongue lashing.

Only John Wolcott's active, visible involvement mitigated the pressures on Lorna during these months. But the regional office resented Lorna even more for hiding behind his coat tails.

"The central problem is short-term versus long-term," Brian said on one of his visits. "Eventually they will realize that two or three quarters may go by until they see the results of this initiative. Then they will see spectacular results and because they live quarter by quarter they will have forgotten all about the cost six months ago."

And they will try to get as much credit as they can, thought Lorna.

Another major problem occurred as a result of their new marketing strategy. They had quietly reduced the number of conference-related guests and had done what they could to encourage individual guests from the target profile they had agreed upon. This had two results.

First, their occupancy went down. This was not helped by one group, which complained to Palmer Hotels directly about not having rooms during a week when the hotel was only running seventy percent occupancy.

Secondly, the Happy Guest Index dropped because the individual guests had higher expectations and were paying a higher rate than the group business. And the individuals were the only ones who were filling in the questionnaires because Lorna and Sarah felt that they would get more useful information. Because the individual guests expected more, the ratings declined. Lorna knew how to manipulate the numbers but she and Brian had agreed that this was a bad idea, since they would not learn anything that would help them improve the services.

chapter XXVIII

Statistics, Beautiful Statistics

During this time Brian had been working an average of two days a month in the hotel. Usually he met with Lorna at the beginning and end of every visit. He also met with Bill to review progress on standards and procedures and certification. The balance of his time he was in the hotel's workplaces meeting with individual staff and counseling managers. His function now was to troubleshoot; to see which aspects of the quality system were dysfunctional, where barriers existed along the chain of service.

In February he taught a course called "Service Innovation" to the Green Mountain Gang to help them learn statistical process control and other more innovative measurement systems for the service industry and the process of solving problems in groups.

"Some of you studied statistics in school or have taken statistics seminars. What is your feeling about statistics?"

"Overly complicated."

"Boring."

"Irrelevant."

"Too academic."

Brian pretended to grimace.

"By the end of the day tomorrow," he said, "you will see how statistics and other measurement tools can be your friend and the friend of your employees. You will see how much data is available to you already and you will understand how to use it to achieve everlasting glory as hoteliers."

He turned over a page in the flip chart. There was a diagram of the chain of service.

"You are hands-on managers. You spend a great deal of time walking around talking with your staff, training them, talking with your guests, listening to people. However, no matter how much you can see, touch, or taste on a daily basis, there is a great deal going on that is invisible as you walk around. That's why, for example, you often consult numbers. What are some examples of numbers that are important to you?"

"Cost of sales."

"Occupancy."

"Forecasts."

"Performance same day last year."

"Food cost."

"Linen count."

"Overtime."

"These are all numbers that tell you more than you can observe or remember," he continued. "They help you make decisions based on more than intuition and experience. You could work very, very hard every day and if you ignored the numbers, your accomplishments might be minimal.

"Unfortunately, most of these numbers have a financial basis.

"Statistical process control is a means of extending these numbers so that they give us a measurement of how we are doing in terms of the quality of our product. It is a scorecard."

Brian looked around the room. "The way we are using statistics in the hotel is twofold," he said. "First, find out what is important to our customers — internal and external. Sarah has done an excellent job of analyzing and profiling our targeted customers. We have thus been able to tell what is important to them in some detail. We know, for example, that a clean room is more important to them than an amenity package. We know that staff attention to them and flexibility is important. We have learned that they do not want food that is too exotic.

"You have analyzed the jobs performed in the hotel and you have diagrammed the chain of service. The first step in the statistical process is finding out what's important — the key quality indicators— and this has been done with the paying guests. Now we need to work upstream through the chain of service to determine what's important to each customer in order for us to provide what's important to the next customer. What are the key quality indicators throughout the enterprise?

"The second step is to determine how well we are meeting customers' needs. The Palmer Happy Guest Index, HGI, gives us some indication of this, but we need much more information than that. For example, it does not ask our guests about some of the aspects of service that are important to them. It compares one hotel to another rather than tracking an individual hotel. It also uses HGI as a means of trying to inspire new and greater performance from general managers. What if the system and facilities simply cannot produce higher HGI ratings? Do you fire the manager? The main problem with HGI is that it doesn't tell us enough, frequently enough and fast enough and from enough of a sample. I am sure that in the future this will change.

"So, statistics tell us: one, what is important to our customer and two, how we're doing. In a market-driven company, these two questions are much more vital to the future of the company than, 'Did I exceed my quota? Did my room attendants average fourteen rooms a day? Are my food costs below twenty-eight percent? or Is my overtime up or down?'

"Statistics should have several characteristics," he said, "and we will endeavor to meet each of these. In the next two days, I will show you how.

"The characteristics are as follows."

Brian turned over a page in the flip chart.

1. Accurate

"Sometimes we are going to be able to get pure scientific data, such as temperature readings in a dishwashing machine or the amount of time it takes to get an order up to a room from room service. This is called quantitative. Other times we will get subjective data, such as employee responsiveness and flexibility. This is called qualitative. In the latter case we will try to get as broad a sample as possible and try to ask the questions in the best possible way to ensure we are getting an accurate picture."

2. Frequent

"Frequency helps us understand how we are doing through different conditions such as weather, ups and downs of the stock market, seasons, etc. It also enables us to spot trends more easily."

3. Easy to get

"We will share the data gathering with many employees. Room service servers will time themselves in getting orders to the rooms. Room attendants will ultimately inspect their own rooms...."

"Hold on, Brian, we are still living in the real world," said Fred. "Why should employees want to inspect their own work? They would fudge on the figures to make whatever point they would want to make."

"At the beginning they might," Brian said. "After a while they will see the benefits in the system. If you manage it well, they will be very happy to help collect data."

The group was extremely skeptical.

4. Neutral and friendly

"By this I mean that the data itself is treated as information with neither good nor bad connotations.

"You are not going to reward or punish your staff or each other on the basis of the data. The data, if it shows a high level of customer dissatisfaction, gives you only one emotion — excitement that you have a system problem to attack."

Brian put the group through a variation of Dr. Deming's funnel experiment, the object of which is to hit the target with a marble. A funnel is fixed over the target and marbles are dropped through it. Often, if the first marble falls wide of the target, the experimenters are tempted to move the funnel. It is better to do nothing but drop more marbles into the funnel and watch a pattern develop.

He showed them a rudimentary control chart and showed them that attention should be focused on data that falls outside the statistical control limits.

5. Fast

"It took you sixty days to get your HGI information. In our data gathering we will get useful information within two or three days, at the most."

6. Consistent

"We will try to ask the same questions in the same way every time we sample our customers. In this manner we can have a reliable comparison of information from one time to the next."

7. Understandable

"Not only should your staff collect the data, they must learn how to read it. You will take this workbook and train each staff person how to use it. Finally, data has to be collected and presented in a form that people can understand and interpret. This is really the essence of this seminar: how to collect, analyze and present the invisible information that tells us how we are doing."

For the rest of the session, Brian helped the group understand how to collect and analyze data, and how to develop rudimentary statistical control charts. Each member of the group drafted a statistical program for their own department and presented it to the group. Brian also reviewed his three-step problem-solving process with them, and each person practiced running a problem-solving session using data.

At the end, Sam stood up and walked up to the front of the room.

"This has been an extremely good two days for all of us. Personally, I take great satisfaction in knowing that we are to become a whole organization of beancounters." He paused while some members of the group clapped and others booed him good-naturedly.

"The exciting thing to me," he began again, "is that we are developing numbers that relate directly to our mission and our driving strategy, and we are going to treat these numbers as guidance, just as we would a compass heading in a boat. They are not good or bad; they simply tell us in what direction we are heading. I learned a great deal from you in these last two days, Brian, and I hope our office can be of help to all of you in the next few months. We have the equipment and the staff to work with you as problems arise. And now, the accounting department has a special surprise for you." A cart of chilled champagne was wheeled in while the group clapped.

Lorna picked up a bottle, wrinkling her nose as she examined it.

"Four dollars and ninety-five cents a bottle," said Sam. "We wanted the best!"

chapter
XXIX

the Mirror

The sales department had developed what Sarah called a "schizophrenic personality." Traditionally, ninety percent of their efforts had been concentrated on sales, bringing the guests in, as opposed to marketing, finding out *who* the guests are. Most directors of sales and marketing were actually directors of sales. They had been trained as salespeople and their lives had been devoted to getting as much business of any hue into whatever hotel they worked for. Many had shifted from one job to another with some frequency. This had little to do with their talent or lack thereof. It had more to do with what Brian called the "Great American hero/villain" syndrome, which laid unlimited faith in the ability of an individual to ride into town and save the settlers. Astute general managers knew that poor sales could be blamed on the directors of sales and that firing them and replacing them with someone else would give the general managers a number of months' grace while they sent out their own résumés.

John Wolcott and other managers of Palmer Hotels felt that the company was missing a golden opportunity by centralizing all its marketing functions. Palmer was really an interesting mixture of products.

It could have one of the best gourmet restaurants in a city, as well as one of the dingiest coffee shops. It had as much Formica as it had walnut paneling.

John thought the very diversity of products could be turned to the company's strategic advantage. Other chains developed a fairly uniform product and had an advantage that they could draw guests from a specific market segment from one city to another in the same manner that McDonald's was McDonald's. Thus, where Marriott, for example, had a strategic advantage of product consistency, Palmer could exploit its strategic advantage of product flexibility. Palmer could benefit from having hotels everywhere that were the best for people who needed to travel to that particular area. Palmer Hotels had the advantage of being able to develop products that were unique to a location.

Another reason for decentralization was that many of the decisions that brought a new guest from, say, Santa Barbara, California, to a specific New York hotel, were actually made in New York, not Santa Barbara. The prospective visitor is told by a friend or relative or a client's secretary in New York that they should stay at the Palmer Madison Avenue. If this was true, then the marketing and sales for the New York hotel could be largely done in New York and the product could be tailored to the New York market because Palmer did not operate with strict product guidelines.

For this reason, John welcomed and encouraged the efforts of Brian and Lorna to add a serious market thrust to the sales office.

Sarah and her staff blossomed with this new attention. She took two crash courses in marketing and read everything she could get her hands on. Her sales staff was still a sales staff but their efforts became much more focused. Their calls were entirely limited to the target market and they took on a new role of gathering data. It was through their efforts that the "Target Market Profile" was developed. As mentioned earlier, this profile drove the renovation program and it drove the writing of standards of service. It answered Brian's first statistical question, "What's important to the end user, our guest?"

The sales and marketing staff also helped answer Brian's second question, "How are we doing in meeting these needs?"

Sarah developed a simple written questionnaire that was religiously given out by the front desk to twenty percent of the customers who fell within the target market profile, asking them to rate the hotel's services in the four most important attributes, as well as writing down any additional comments they might have. Because the bell staff who roomed the guest and the clerk who checked them out all stated the importance of the questionnaire to the "continuous improvement of our services," the response rate on the questionnaires was an unheard-of forty percent.

Brian showed Sarah how to develop run charts that measured guest satisfaction using these weekly snapshots. The run charts were posted in several prominent areas in the hotel and employees were encouraged to write comments on the chart.

The sales staff augmented this effort by conducting "leisure time" interviews in which they interviewed random target market profile guests about the hotel's services and particularly what these guests would like to see added to the hotel's services. The concierge, the front desk clerks, the bell staff and the floor supervisors in housekeeping were trained in the same activity. The results of the questions were carefully tabulated on a weekly basis with a summary posted on the board as well.

Finally, some of the focus groups were audiotaped. The tapes were played in the departmental staff meetings and the staff encouraged to comment.

At Brian's suggestion, a scanner that could be attached to the Apple Macintosh in the training department was purchased. A software program was purchased that enabled the computer to write, read, and interpret questionnaires. Lorna buried the cost in the construction budget, with John's acquiescence. The sales staff grew by two people and there was a small amount of overtime. Once in a while a guest or restaurant customer would complain about being "asked to death." In general, however, the effort was spread among so many people that its cost was nominal. For most customers, moreover, the results were very positive. They enjoyed being asked.

Thus, the hotel became familiar with its targeted market. It knew who the targeted guests were, what their needs were and it had a scorecard by which to judge the overall satisfaction of these guests. What it didn't know was how the "internal customers" felt about the services provided to them.

For the next two months, Brian and his disciples, Sarah and Sam, worked closely with each department in setting up a statistical control process. Each department's requirements were different and the team found a challenge each day.

"Each department, in effect, produces a product," Brian told the team at an early morning breakfast session. "As with the guest services, we will first determine what's important about the product to the department's customers and second, figure out a way to measure how the department is doing in producing the product. The raw numbers will be converted into charts so that all staff can read them. This means boiling down the information into numbers that indicate performance on a scale.

"We will start, in most cases, with compliance to standard. This is a yes/no decision. Either the performance was up to standard or it wasn't. We will take a snapshot and get a mass of yes/no data. We will then convert this data to a range of numbers, say from seventy to eighty. An eighty becomes our upper and seventy becomes our lower control limits."

"Will it be percentage of compliance?" asked Sam. "In some cases," Brian said, "but let's wait and see."

chapter
XXX

Clean, Well-maintained Rooms

Logic dictated that the first step was in housekeeping. Every survey determined that a clean, well-maintained room was of primary importance to the target market profile. Every member of the Green Mountain Gang felt that the room inspections in their present form were wasteful of personnel and disrespectful of the room attendants. But no one could figure out how to get rid of them. The executive housekeeper, Ruth Schmidt, had tried an experiment by not inspecting any rooms for five days. The rooms were dirtier than ever at the end of the time and it took two weeks to bring them back up to status quo ante. There was a constant tug of war between the floor supervisors and the room attendants. The strong supervisors chased the room attendants and made them come back and clean the rooms. The weak supervisors fixed the problems themselves. There was resentment and animosity on both sides.

Brian first talked the floor supervisors into marking down compliance (yes or no, item by item, room by room) on a checklist that gradually grew to over three hundred items.

As he predicted, the room inspection took longer and longer and there was a significant difference between the observations of one supervisor and another. The supervisors complained that they were so busy writing down data that they could not correct the problems. If anything, they said, the rooms were getting more out of compliance each day.

Also, as he predicted they were soon swimming in data. Three hundred items, times two hundred inspections times seven days, produced one hundred forty-nine thousand and eight hundred bits of information in a single week. Working closely with Ruth, they developed a form that could be read by the scanner. The computer, in turn, produced a weekly run chart that showed an overall percentage of acceptable rooms by attribute. The room inspections were devoted to four areas: cleanliness, maintenance, completeness of supplies and amenities, and placement.

Because the target market profile had rated these in this order of importance, the overall index weighed these attributes, giving less weight to placement than to completeness, for example.

The program also enabled the housekeeping staff to zoom in on a specific attribute, or sub-attribute, such as the mirrors in the bathroom, and determine if there was what Brian called "instability in the process of production" and what Ruth called "sloppy work."

In one of her daily briefings to the housekeeping staff, Ruth explained the process and posted the chart for the first month. She explained that the chart did not show which room attendant did what and that it was neither bad nor good. The staff were skeptical but nearly everyone crowded up to look at the chart after the meeting. A marker was hung from the bulletin board and employees were encouraged to write comments.

A scribbled comment the first week inadvertently triggered the first step upstream through the chain of service.

"What do you expect? The sheets are bad," said the comment.

Ruth asked around and found out that the comment was triggered by the fact that the room attendants apparently were receiving sheets from the laundry that were either dirty or ripped and had to be returned.

Ruth asked the room attendants to record each time the problem occurred and collected the data for a week. This sample indicated that an astronomical twenty-five percent of linen of all types was unusable. The team set up a statistical program to continuously measure this problem.

After a few days, it was clear that the problem was chronic and subject to only minor fluctuations. "This is a classic case of a process that is under statistical control. It is stable," Brian said.

"I'm happy for you, Brian," joked Ruth. "It still stinks."

Brian took time out from the statistical process to create a flowchart that showed the process of production of clean room linen. He then met with the laundry staff and presented both the flow chart and the statistical chart to them in one of their weekly meetings. The group was extremely shy. They were not sure who Brian was or what new form of punishment he represented. Fortunately, the laundry manager committed a full hour to the meeting and the meeting was held informally in the laundry room with the noisiest equipment shut down.

"You know," began Brian, "one of my jobs at home is to take the garbage out. I want to do a good job in this. My wife takes the responsibility for shopping because she works near a grocery store and I hate to shop. A few weeks ago my wife bought garbage bags that had holes in both ends. Could I do my job well? Was it her fault? Was it my fault? Was it the store's fault? We always want to do a good job, but at times we are prevented from doing it because the system is wrong."

There was some discussion in which he realized that the laundry staff were fully cognizant of the problems created for the room attendants and that there was a genuine desire to solve the problem. He then presented the flowchart and asked them to help him identify places where the problem might be occurring. There was a very good discussion about this. Finally, he asked what they felt could be done about the problem. There were a number of suggestions from the group.

Following the meeting he spoke at length with the laundry manager and they decided on a plan of implementation that included further study in some areas and the need to get approval for others.

Brian and the laundry manager established a timeline for action and made a copy of Brian's notes, which were put on the bulletin board next to the run chart and the flow chart. Already someone had made a note on the flowchart with the words "macinaria flojo" — poor machinery — next to one of the dryers. The laundry manager agreed to check on the comment.

The run chart started showing improvement even before the laundry meeting, in part because the room attendants began separating out the unusable linen and putting it in bags, thus taking it out of circulation. It appeared that the unusable linen had been making an endless circle through the laundry up to the floors and back to the laundry. Stopping the circle was an added complexity for the room attendants but Ruth wisely increased her staffing slightly so as to reduce the actual number of rooms each person cleaned. Within three weeks she was able to bring the staffing down to its normal level when the percentage of poor linen dropped to fifteen percent.

"Heck, that's as good as we're going to get," Ruth said to Brian. "Let's stop counting and worry about the rooms." Brian convinced her to continue.
"If clean unripped linen is important to helping you provide the guests with clean rooms, then we should continue sampling this product forever. Over time, however, we can reduce the sample."

Ruth reluctantly agreed and week by week the percentage inched downward. Brian continued to play an active role in the problem-solving process, faithfully attending each of the laundry meetings. He backed away from active leadership of the meetings but did coach the manager in the problem-solving process.

In eight weeks the percentage had dropped to four with the upper control limits eight and the lower control limits zero. It was an easy success, and one that had substantial payoff in hard cash.

chapter
XXXI

Coffee Shop

The Green Mountain Gang decided that the statistical trio should put the coffee shop under "statistical control" next.

Brian had conducted an employee climate survey every three months and the results showed the morning coffee shop staff had the highest level of discontent of any department.

Sarah had also determined that a good breakfast ranked very high in the target market profile and that guests did not rate their product very highly. The surveys of breakfast and lunch guests determined that sixty-five percent were concerned about speed as a key quality indicator. Most guests did not feel that the speed of service was satisfactory.

The statistical process in the dining room was helped enormously by electronics. The "point of sale" equipment purchased as part of the renovation had a feature that could measure speed. It could tell how long it took for an order to come out of the kitchen and it could tell the overall length of the meal period. The dining room manager could usually tell whether the guest was in a hurry or was in the dining room for a leisurely breakfast or lunch. She would then track the speed of meals for the people for whom speed was most important.

Sam conducted classes on elementary statistics for the dining room and kitchen staff. Characteristically, he made the class fun by giving analogies from people's everyday lives. He asked them to time their trips to work for a week and he also asked them to count the number of times their children and spouses asked for money. He then charted this data.

By the time he introduced the first run chart showing the speed of service over a ten-day period of time, they knew how to read and analyze the chart. He asked them to tell him what caused the variation and to write in their comments on the chart. They saw that speed of service was a function of day-of-week, the number of customers served, and staffing. Brian had helped the dining room manager and the coffee shop chef plot all these factors for the same time period so that the group could see the correlation.

The coffee shop began collecting very specific customer feedback from the guests for whom speed was important. They devised a very simple questionnaire for each group. Instead of asking, "Did you enjoy your meal?" the wait staff asked, "Is there anything you would like us to do differently the next time you are here, Mr. (Ms.)_____?" The server then noted down the comment on the questionnaire form. Sarah ran two interview skills training sessions for the wait staff to help them feel confident in asking the questions. She had them role play various situations. So as not to wear out the question, it was asked of all guests only once a week.

Working with Brian and Sam, the coffee shop and kitchen management designed flow charts for the entire chain of service. Once this was completed, all available staff from purchasing, the kitchen and the dining room met once a week, mid-morning for an hour, to review data and apply Brian's problem-solving process to ways of improving the production process.

The meetings were stormy at first and Brian ran them to prevent fatal loss of blood. Both the kitchen and the service staff felt that they had been prevented from success by the other.

"You never get the orders right. You think 'over easy' means poached."

"Half the orders sit for ten minutes before you pick them up."

"Why do you give us yesterday's bacon?"

"You steal each other's orders."

"You have a memory like Steinbrunner!"

"You never say 'please' or 'thank you.' You never use our names. You must have flunked the T.I.G.E.R. course."

Brian let the first session run like this for twenty minutes before he gently reminded them that they had a common problem, which could only be worked out together.

Slowly and hesitantly, they began tackling the process problems. They found little steps that could smooth out communication and the flow of services. Some of these improvements cost money for purchases of new equipment and training time. At least half the improvements cost virtually nothing in terms of capital expenditures. As improvements were identified, management found itself changing the flow charts, rewriting the standards and procedures, and retraining staff as the changes were made. The chef began conducting a regular class on the menu items. He held cooking demonstrations and taste tests. As new menu items were added, management conducted simulations, a process they had learned during the "Training For Results" course.

"Measure, fix, train," Brian was fond of saying, "then measure again."

If anything, the results came much faster than they had in housekeeping. Positive guest comments jumped almost at once. The lines at breakfast disappeared. The speed of service increased by a full thirty percent. Payroll increased sharply and then slowly declined. Food costs declined, as did the food and beverage inventories.

And the coffee shop's popularity began to take off. Even during the traditionally slow month of August, more than half the breakfast diners came from the neighborhood. In September, for the first time in recorded history, the food and beverage department recorded an operating profit!

chapter
XXXII

Housekeeping's New Tricks

Until this time, Ruth had not analyzed the ideal system of cleaning a room. Her standards and procedures were very complete but did not dictate what the housekeeping staff should carry into the room when entering or how many trips they should take to their carts. She observed that each room attendant had a different system. It seemed unlikely that she was going to get the team to change unless they could see the logic in changing.

She talked with Brian about the problem.

Brian suggested that she confine the new procedures to the newly renovated rooms. Maybe the newness would help the room attendants accept the change, even though the cleaning procedures would be substantially similar.

With two of the floor supervisors, Ruth spent two afternoons in one of the new rooms. They worked out what they felt was the optimum method of cleaning. They were able to reduce the number of trips into the room from eight to six, by carefully figuring out what a person should carry in and out with each trip. Brian observed the last trip and made a simple chart of the process on the training department's computer.

He also thought a great deal about the process that evening and realized they had made a mistake.

The next day, he suggested that Ruth go through the whole process again with a team of room attendants. Six room attendants were randomly selected and the entire process was repeated, this time with two full days allocated for the effort. First, they walked around the room and discussed various aspects of the cleaning of the room. They looked at the checklist for a clean room and added some items. Ruth explained that she had determined that in one month, one room attendant could walk nearly fourteen miles more than another if they didn't use the correct routine. "That's the length of Manhattan," she said "or two hundred and eighty blocks. Now, if I set out to walk the length of Manhattan, how many coffee breaks could you take by the time I got to the end?"

Brian winced. The argument should be that they will be cleaning the rooms better, he thought.

By the end of the second day, they had arrived at a system that reduced the trips in and out of the room to five and the total walking distance down to sixty-five yards per room. The last thing the room attendant did was to carefully walk around the room, checking everything and testing light bulbs.

At the end of that day, Brian went back to the training department with the executive housekeeper and showed her how to do the flow chart on the computer.

The next day she gave each team member a copy of the flow chart. Each of them made up a room using the new system, while she and the two floor supervisors observed. Following the "Training For Results" format, she conducted a critique after each person practiced.

For three long days, the six room attendants practiced. Ruth then asked them to use the new system on the "old" rooms. "This will give you plenty of time to be ready for the new rooms. I am going to repeat the practice sessions next week after you have had a chance to clean a few rooms using the new system. Finally, if there are any problems with the system, please let me know about it when we get together next week."

Ruth was astonished that there was no rolling of eyes or grumbling. She realized that everyone benefited by standardizing the "process of production," the guests, management, staff and the union. She also felt that the nine of them had formed a much closer bond. The following week each of the six room attendants was observed by either Ruth or one of the floor supervisors while they cleaned two rooms. The same critique process was used. The room attendants became more efficient in the new process, and it was clear that they had been actually using the new system. Ruth repeated the process with this team for three more weeks.

Next, Ruth personally trained each of the other floor supervisors in the new process. This was also time-consuming and they were surprisingly resistant to the change. All of them had been room attendants for years and they had done an excellent job or they would not have been promoted. She found it took more than a day to train two people and she began to despair that she would never be able to train the rest of the room attendants.

This turned out to be easier than she expected, however. All the room attendants were now retrained by the floor supervisors in small groups. The members of the original team were relieved of having to clean rooms for three weeks and helped out as "teachers." The "teachers" would demonstrate the new procedures and then observe closely while the "students" practiced, one by one. At the end of the second day, Ruth or her assistant observed each person making up a room and critiqued them afterward.

The process was slow and time-consuming. Ruth spent more than one hundred thirty-two hours in the process. It was also expensive in terms of payroll. There was some grumbling about having a floor supervisor observe performance once a week. The results, however, showed that the process would easily pay for itself within a few months.

The floor supervisors now reduced the number of rooms inspected each day to fifty percent. The inspections were much more thorough and the floor supervisors kept much better data. The entire staff could see the percentage of acceptable rooms creeping upward on the run chart.

A daily review helped the floor supervisors look at trends within the "big picture." They could tell, for example, if bathtubs were not getting cleaned as well as they should be, or if linen was getting frayed or if there were dripping faucets.

Ruth reviewed the data carefully and led each daily briefing with a discussion of the chart. If there was a trend either way, she would comment on it and encourage feedback from the staff. In the weekly meeting, the entire housekeeping staff began working together on the system's problems.

For a time, the floor supervisors continued the process of chasing down individual room attendants and bringing them back to non-compliant rooms. Gradually, the data showed that this practice could be abandoned. Four months after her first strategy session with Brian, it had become clear to Ruth that the room attendants were inspecting their own work.

The results were extremely rewarding. Guest comments concerning room cleanliness and maintenance continued to improve. Room inspections were reduced to a thorough inspection for every room once a week. The floor supervisors focused their time on interviewing guests, solving problems, analyzing data, training, and studying the "upstream" causes of situations that hindered production process. They stopped being a police force and focused instead on supporting the room attendants. They worked closely with the maintenance department when it was determined that a number of maintenance problems were preventable if detected earlier. One floor supervisor left the hotel for an assistant housekeeper job. Another was promoted to the accounting department. Neither were replaced.

Most important for Ruth Schmidt was that she was spending much less time fighting fires. There were simply fewer fires to fight.

"In the old days, " she told John Wolcott on one of his frequent visits to the back-of-the-house, "you could always tell when there was a full moon. The different ethnic groups in my department would be at each other's throats. There was constant turmoil. They are now united by a common cause — the perfect room. I always loved my work, but I never would have guessed that it could be so totally creative."

chapter XXXIII
Triumph

Almost exactly a year after the first meeting in Vermont, the Green Mountain Gang met again. To Lorna it seemed a miracle that the group's membership was unchanged.

As luck would have it, the weather was just as beautiful as it had been the year before. The inn's food was as spectacular as they remembered it.

The meeting was a two-day celebration of their achievements, as well as a planning process for the future. They knew so much more than they had the year before! They had a much better understanding of their two markets — guests and staff — and they knew how the chain of service was performing in most of the key areas. They had a clear idea of where the bottlenecks, pressure points and other problems were.

Most important, they were confident in their ability to solve these problems. Brian added relatively little new knowledge and skills to the session. He said very little. Each member of the group had a facilitation role and helped the large group or small "buzz groups" work through problems. Brian sat in on as many sessions as he could and always critiqued the facilitator afterward. They worked out solutions to a number of problems that had confronted them.

At the end of the session, John Wolcott talked quietly and with great emotion.

He told them how much they meant to him and Maria Luisa, how much he had personally grown in the last year. He pointed out that the cost of the quality effort could not possibly be justified in monetary terms yet, and the year's results were going to be flat, with revenues and expenses both rising in equal proportion. "In a few months, however, you will see numbers that will knock your socks off. Your concerted effort to reduce costs without harming the guests is really paying off," he said. The group cheered. "As the numbers start getting better, however, I feel that we, as owners, should share a healthy portion of the profit with you and the staff. For this reason, my family has developed a profit-sharing trust. The trust will reward tenure in the hotel. The longer a person stays, the higher percentage he or she will have upon retirement."

He thanked the stunned group again and turned the floor over to Lorna.

She spoke only briefly, she thanked Brian. "And John," she said, "if you really mean profit sharing, you'll never get rid of us. We are deeply grateful to you." She thanked the group individually, one by one, making humorous comments about each person and praising their achievements.

"I think we are sometimes so overwhelmed by the amount we have yet to do, we forget how far we have come in fourteen short months. So, in closing, I would like to read a letter from Mrs. Grandmaison, from Chicago. She stays with us fairly often, as you know.

"Dear Lorna," she read from a piece of elegant stationery, "I just want to thank you and your staff for all the little things they did for me on my last visit. As you know, I travel a great deal and I am afraid I have become somewhat jaded. I have always liked the Palmer Madison Avenue Hotel but, candidly, it was sometimes a struggle to get basic needs met.

"In this last visit, I noticed that there seems to be a spirit about the hotel that was missing before. It was almost like a mysterious, joyful glow. Employees constantly used my name. They were able to help me in little ways I never thought possible. They even remembered that I like a room away from the Avenue. The staff seemed to be much kinder and more thoughtful toward one another. All the services, the cleanliness of the room, and the food were better than I remember them. I am not sure what you are doing, Lorna, but for the three days I stayed in the hotel, I can only describe the service as perfect."

Lorna's strong Yankee voice quavered, her eyes no longer seeing the paper. She stood vainly trying to see her audience in the late afternoon sun. Her eyes blinked and she looked frail and awkward.

John stood and shook her hand. Slowly at first, each of the members of the team stood and walked toward Lorna as if pulled by a giant magnet toward this small figure. Each waited in turn, to shake her hand and then shook the hands of each of their partners.

chapter XXXIV

Author's Note

This book was written to help you realize that to bring about change in our industry will take courage, creativity and persistence. It is also intended to inspire you to think beyond the sacred traditions and truisms of the industry. The essence of hotel greatness is and always will be that happy conspiracy between the staff and the guest. Management is the preservation and support of that conspiracy, breaking down anything which hinders that magic point of contact.

The purpose of the epilogue (which is based on dozens of real life experiences) is to try to stem the unnecessary shredding or disruption of hundreds of thousands of hotel careers now taking place by misguided, short-sighted owners and hotel corporations. It took the Green Mountain Gang a long time to develop a set of common values with their owner. But Palmer Hotels never bought it. Without synergy between management corporations, owners and the hotels themselves, the industry will continue to waste careers, money and confuse our customers.

chapter XXXV

Epilogue

Two weeks later, the small plane carrying John and Maria Luisa from San Juan to St. Barthélemy disappeared without a trace. Lorna was in a meeting with the Green Mountain Gang when one of the phone operators burst into the room sobbing and blurted out the news. Lorna, pale but calm, closed the meeting and immediately called a friend at CBS. The friend confirmed the story and Lorna immediately took a cab to the couple's apartment.

The Wolcott girls were both in the apartment when she arrived. Lorna held the girls for a long time, three forlorn figures in the middle of the vast kitchen. Relatives began arriving and stood awkwardly, talking to each other quietly.

Events happened with dizzying speed after that. The family decided to sell the hotel and instructed Palmer to put the hotel under a strict austerity program. The renovation program was stopped and the regional controller moved into the hotel. He looked very carefully through the books and discovered Brian's fees and expenses, as well as the fees of the training consultants. In fourteen months, he told Lorna maliciously, she had spent over five hundred thousand dollars in fees, expenses, extra salary, and overtime. Lorna was ordered to cancel Brian's contract and cut overtime.

The Palmer Hotels' headquarters management staff thought that CTX Corporation should buy the hotel. Unfortunately, there was a secret pipeline between the Palmer regional office and CTX financial staff. All the "excesses" came to light in the board meeting in which the Palmer executives presented their plan for the purchase.

Palmer realized that they would need to present the next board meeting with "new news," or any purchase plan was dead. The most dramatic new news they could give the board was the termination of the general manager.

Lorna was given her notice twenty-eight days after John and Maria Luisa had disappeared. She had been told by several people that the move was imminent and was well prepared when the regional vice president of operations came to her office.

"You are a good manager," he said, "but I'm afraid you are over your head in this job. The hotel is really out of control. The costs of your so-called quality initiative are beyond my comprehension and the fact that you, in effect, cooked the books to hide some of these costs is totally inexcusable. We have tried to help you but...."

Lorna was given a full year's severance pay and was allowed to stay in the hotel during the entire time if she wished. She didn't wish.

In her last meeting with the full staff she thanked them for all they had given her personally. She urged them to continue the systems that had been set up with so much effort.

After she finished there was a standing ovation. Some staff wept unashamedly.

Johnny DelGado stood up and told her that the hotel was going to sorely miss her and that they were not going to let any new manager set a different course of action. He was cheered for his speech.

At the very end of the ceremony, one of the room attendants came up to the front of the room with a small box and presented it to Lorna. "We want to thank you, Miss Lorna, for your help in making our job better and respecting us. You are a true Tiger." Lorna opened the box and took out a small brass plaque.

"A Señorita Lorna Johnson con mil gracias," it said. "Un Lindo Requerdo."

A beautiful memory.

About the Author

David A. Borden is the founder of Victoria International Corporation, which trains business and industry supervisors in human relations skills. He first became involved in the hospitality industry in the early 1970s when Laurance Rockefeller asked him to develop a system to train staff for the opening of his Cerromar Beach Hotel in Puerto Rico.

While working with Mr. Rockefeller, Mr. Borden and his partners created numerous innovative training programs for hotel front line staff, supervisors and management, which he implemented in luxury hotel chains in the United States.

Since 1978, VIC partners have trained staff in 73 newly opened hotels and resorts and have helped improve customer service for 400 other hotels in 36 countries.

In the mid-1980s, Mr. Borden turned to Total Quality and studied with W. Edwards Deming and others. During this period, Mr. Borden began work on this book, "Perfect Service—Creating the Best Hotel in New York," which addresses the challenges the hospitality industry faces in implementing the concepts of total quality. Presently, he is working with a few hotel chains to fundamentally redesign the way hotels are managed.

Mr. Borden lives with his wife, Nancy, in Boston and Singapore. He has 7 children and 2 grandchildren.

Mr. Borden may be reached at:
Victoria International Corporation
187 West Brookline Street
Boston, MA 02118
Tel: (617) 247-4100   Fax: (617) 247-0038

Discover the secrets of hotels with successful TQM programs ... Plus action ideas for making your own efforts pay off!

Does your hotel's quality drive fall short of your expectations? Maybe it's time for some practical techniques instead of lofty theories. *Total Quality In Hospitality* is the only monthly newsletter that takes you inside hotels where quality efforts are paying off and reveals their secrets for success. You save time and money spent on frustrating efforts that don't pan out.

You find out how other hotels foster innovations, build teamwork, reduce costs and boost guest satisfaction. Upcoming issues will bring you inside details on how to exceed guest expectations without exceeding your budget ... ways to tie TQ efforts to higher profits ... techniques to measure quality, create fierce loyalty on the part of your guests and generate meaningful guest feedback ... how to overcome management indifference to TQM ... red flags that warn you of leadership problems at your hotel ... and much more!

Total Quality In Hospitality bridges the gap between concept and reality of implementing TQM in your hotel — we guarantee it! If you don't believe *Total Quality In Hospitality* brings you quality boosting ideas worth many times the subscription price, simply cancel at any time in the coming year and receive a full refund.

Raise the quality level in hundreds of areas throughout your hotel ... areas that have a direct positive impact on guest satisfaction and profits. Subscribe to *Total Quality In Hospitality* today.

Magna Publications, Inc
2718 Dryden Drive, Madison, WI 53704.
Telephone: 800-433-0499; Fax: 608/246-3597.

Prevent Lawsuits and Protect Your Hotel's Bottom Line

Just trying to keep up with all the laws, court cases, rules and regulations affecting your guests and employees can be overwhelming. Yet, you can't afford these developments when legal costs for even a "minor" incident can run into the thousands ... and that doesn't include the damage to your reputation. How can you fight back?

Subscribe to *Hospitality Law*, the concise monthly briefing devoted exclusively to helping you reduce the risk of lawsuits. It's easy to understand, with no "legalese." And, in 20 minutes a month, it keeps you up to date on legal developments affecting hotels. You get an ongoing supply of strategies for preventing crimes against guests ... practical advice for avoiding claims of sexual harassment, wrongful discharge, discrimination and other current employment trouble spots ... ways to minimize risk of dram shop liability, updates on ADA and family leave act compliance ... checklists for swimming pool and exercise room safety ... techniques for handling overbooking complaints, contract disputes and trademark infringement claims ... and dozens more tools to reduce your chances of getting sued.

And you can subscribe with our risk-free guarantee: If you find *Hospitality Law* doesn't meet your expectations, simply cancel at any time in the coming year and get 100% of your subscription refunded — no questions asked!

Make no mistake: Today's litigation-crazed climate will only intensify in coming months. Protect yourself by subscribing to *Hospitality Law* now, your best "insurance" for reducing risk and preventing costly litigation.

Magna Publications, Inc
2718 Dryden Drive, Madison, WI 53704.
Telephone: 800-433-0499; Fax: 608/246-3597.